RIGHTLY DIVIDING THE WORD OF TRUTH

II TIMOTHY 2:15 "STUDY TO SHEW THYSELF APPROVED UNTO GOD, A WORKMAN THAT NEEDED NOT TO BE ASHAMED, RIGHTLY DIVIDING THE WORD OF TRUTH."

The genie god.©

Hebrews 10:31 it is a fearful thing to fall into the hands of the living God.

Written by: Christopher E. Howe

This book is dedicated to our grandchildren, present and future. To assist you in your walk with God, and to experience him on a deeper level.

you are loved.

This book is also dedicated to anyone who has a true desire to rightly divide the word of truth and live their life Gods way.

All scripture references are from the King James Version of the bible. The scripture references are bold, italicized, or underlined for emphasis and do not reflect a change in scripture.

Index

Introduction

Is not a Fearful God
Patriotism
Treasure
Pride
Pride Movement
Gender Identity
Abortion
Bible or TV
Selective Judgements
Faith or Fear
Credentials and Accreditations
Treasure

INTRODUCTION

Galatians 5:16 This I say then, Walk in the Spirit, and ye shall not fulfill the lust of the flesh

We have come to a time in our lives that the word Christian has many different meanings and understandings. There have been many who are not saved who call themselves Christians and there are those who have been saved, who have accepted Jesus Christ as their personal Savior that have refused to follow the bible.

The bible is the foundational book of our Christian walk. Most choose not to believe it for what it says. Most reject it. The bible tells us that the natural man, (the lost man on his way to eternity in a lake of fire because he keeps rejecting Jesus Christ) CANNOT understand the things of God. The bible is spiritually revealed to a person by the Holy Spirit a natural man (lost man) does not have the Holy Spirit living in him.

Then there is what the bible calls the Carnal man.
Carnal simply defined is: worldly. This is the person
who is saved, knows they are going to heaven, but who
is walking in the ways of the world. They are the ones
that if you place them in the world next to the lost you
will not be able to tell them apart. These are the ones
who will put on the hypocritical look and be very
judgmental. These are called in the bible Lukewarm
Christians.

The intent of this book is to show how far from the bible
the children of God have drifted. How, in a lot of areas
we have been led astray by false teachers, and false
doctrine. Mostly it will show our refusal to adhere to the
Word of God and apply it to our lives.

This book most likely will upset some, though that is
never my intention, I believe it may also show some
people how we as Christians need to start living for
Jesus and bringing hope to the lost and dying world. It
is also my intention to show Christians that if we repent
of our sinful ways that God will hear, he will answer,
and he will forgive, and our nation can be healed.

We must think also about what kind of a nation are we
leaving for our children and our Grandchildren. The
world is in the chaos it is in because Christians have
turned from the bible. They have turned to traditions,
and what people say, think, or do they have stopped
reading their bible and let the television be their guide.
They have accepted ungodliness in their hearts, which

has been allowed in their homes. This ungodliness continues to go with them to their churches, and to their workplaces.

The bible is very clear that if God's people, HIS PEOPLE, will turn from their wicked ways, then God can and will heal the heart, heal the church, and heal the nation. Once healing has been restored and God has been put first, the gospel can get out. Once the gospel is out and keeps getting out than revival can happen, it really can, the bible says it will.

As you proceeded in this book you will have to make a choice to either believe the bible for what it says, or do not, that choice is yours. Each chapter of this book will identify different areas in our lives where God is only called upon to be a genie and not called upon to be God.

The only time people refer to God in society and in a lot of churches today is when they either want something, or things go wrong in their lives. Other than that God is nowhere to be found in their lives. People, especially Christians living in a carnal state they want a genie god, they want a god that only comes out when they really need something form him then they want him to back into that bottle and stay there until the next time something happens. In this case the bottle is the bible, and the genie is God. Christians do not want a God that convicts them of their sins, they do not want to feel guilty for not telling the lost they are going to Hell. They don't want to make the changes in their sinful lifestyles as they have been very custom to what they have. They want a dead faith as the bible talks about. It talks about a faith without works is dead. Most Christians are very comfortable in this state.

If you choose to get mad at me for writing this book, I am ok with that, I love you and want you to experience the ultimate power and not judgement of God on your lives. In the preceding chapters, I have lived in my life during my prodigal years. I did not experience the ultimate love of God on my life. That true intimate relationship as I am enjoying today.

Yes, this world will fall apart, yes serving God will cost you, it only cost you worldly things and will never, ever cost you spiritual things. No one or nothing can take that from us. Remember it is a FEARFUL thing for a Christian to fall into the hands of the living God.

IS NOT A FEARFUL GOD

Hebrews 10:31 It is a fearful thing to fall into the hands of the living God.

As Christians we must realize that there are consequences for our decisions. Yes, we are free from the eternal punishment of sin, which is eternity in a Lake of Fire, but there are things in the bible that God expects us to do as Christians to live for him. The entire complete purpose for us to live for God and show him in our lives is to bring honor and glory to him.

We bring Honor and glory to God by telling others about Jesus and what he did for us and them on the cross. Without that we and the lost have nothing. We as Christians must understand that the lost world, without Jesus has absolutely no hope in anything or anyone. Since Jesus is the only hope for a lost soul, it is our responsibility to tell that person about Jesus and offer them hope. How can we ever expect them to accept Jesus Christ as their personal Saviour, if we as Christians are not living like Jesus is first and foremost in our lives.

The more I study my bible the deeper the Lord takes me. I told the folks in church the other day, that reading the bible is not an easy task. It requires a discipline. It requires effort, it requires one to be intentional. When you look at life there has never been one thing invented, one successful business made, without there being a discipline to stick with it and make adjustments to get to that success. Sure, there have been those that may have cheated or stole their success, but that success has never lived long. If you want a life focused on God, you must be intentional about living for God.

God holds us as his children accountable for our actions. The bible tells us that we will all give an answer for ourselves to God for the choice we make. God values obedience. Obedience is what strengthens our faith. Most of the time God wants us to obey without knowing the outcome.

If you believe the promises of God, if you believe the bible, it is very clear that God will meet all our needs. If we obey him, then the responsibility falls back on him to meet our needs especially when we don't see a way for them to get met. That is what he does, that is who God is.

It is equally as important that we as Christians understand that when we chose to disobey that there will be consequences. As we will see in this chapter it is a fearful thing for Christians to fall into the hands of the living God. the bible tells us that the Lord chastens, he punishes those whom he loves. Like a child is punished by the parents for their disobedience, so must God as our heavenly father punish us when we disobey.

Let's look now at some verses in the bible about the punishment from God. Gods' punishment is for his children, not the lost, for their disobedience. Remember the lost are already condemned, they are already on their way to a godless damnation for eternity where they will be cast alive in the lake of fire for all eternity, unless they see or hear Jesus in and from you. God does not focus on punishing them, he punishes us, his children, because he loves us.

Hebrews 10:26-31 For if we sin wilfully after that we have received the knowledge of the truth, there remaineth no more sacrifice for sins, But a certain fearful looking for of judgment and fiery indignation, which shall devour the adversaries. He that despised Moses' law died without mercy under two or three witnesses: Of how much sorer punishment, suppose ye, shall he be thought worthy, who hath trodden under foot the Son of God, and hath counted the blood of the covenant, wherewith he was sanctified, an unholy thing, and hath done despite unto the Spirit of grace? For we know him that hath said, Vengeance belongeth unto me, I will recompense, saith the Lord. And again, The Lord shall judge his people. It is a fearful thing to fall into the hands of the living God.

 The God of the bible is not the god the world wants. The world, and carnal Christians wan a god that meets all their needs, that gives them everything they ask for, and allows them to do whatever they want to do. This is the most common god. I call him a genie god.

When we as Christians get into difficult situations, and we need immediate answers we call on God. The Lost world will do this also. Just watch an Atheist jump off an airplane and his parachute fails to open, I bet he then calls on God. Yes, the bible does tell us that God will supply all out need, but it does not stop there he says according to his riches in glory. We must be seeking God to have the God of the bible leading our lives.

After we call on God and our situations seem to settle down, we then go back to our normal routine. We then go back to a life led by our selfish pride. We in essence put God back in the bottle and put him on the shelf until the next time we mess up again and need him. This book will highlight many areas in our live where we only want God to do what we want him to do. Where we only want God to grant us three wishes, and then go away.

The God of the bible is a God to be feared when we mess up. He is a judging God, he is a chastening God, and he is more than anything a loving God. No one wants to be chastened, and we will at times run from this chastening. We often forget that one day we will all, individually have to stand before the God of the bible and answer for ourselves. The god that we want in our lives is a god that will work for us, he is a god who will obey us, this again is not the God of the bible.

Do you want your nation, your life, your children's lives to be the best it can be, then we must do it and go back to the God of the bible and get rid of our genie god. To do this one must submit to God and die to self. Submission is a voluntary action to let God lead your life. All God wants from his children is for them to trust him unconditionally by doing what he says without knowing the outcome, knowing that he will work it all out.

For if we sin wilfully after that we have received the knowledge of the truth, there remaineth no more sacrifice for sins, what a powerful statement made here. This says that we can sin willingly. I believe we all commit sins with intention at the moment we sin. I remember in my prodigal years how I was working for a national beverage company and I needed money. I filled the soda machines which required me to collect the cash. I would then enter everything into the computer and put the cash in the safe. There were times I needed cash so I would manipulate the computer and take the extra cash that was not registered in the computer. I did not initially set out to do this, I did think and dwell on it. Then at the moment of the decision it was an intentional willful decision I made to sin. If you look back on your life and every time you fell into sin that moment you got to where you had to make a choice you wilfully chose to sin. The bible tells us in James, **James 1:15 Then when lust hath conceived, it bringeth forth sin: and sin, when it is finished, bringeth forth death.** Every sin starts with lust, every sin is a willful choice.

Jesus died for our sins on cross. His sacrifice saves us and removes the eternal punishment for our sins. This verse is telling us that once we have received his gift of salvation there is nothing else needed to pay for our sins. Many people take salvation and use it to say that they can live however they want to and there will be no punishments. This mindset falls in line with the topic of this book. The saved of the world living in the world who have a genie god serving them will say I'm saved so I can do what I want, and I will still go to Heaven. Yes, that is true, that once a person is saved, they are sealed with the Holy Spirit. Yes, it is also true that we have liberty to do certain things in our lives. The liberty, freedom, that we have in Christ is a liberty from sin so we can serve God not liberty to have a genie god serve us.

There are no more sacrifices that can be made for the sins of the one that is a child of God. That sacrifice was made at Calvary. There are however consequences to our sins. Once we get saved, we receive the knowledge of truth, if we choose to ignore that knowledge that is fine, however there will be a price to pay. The bible guarantees this. We will see as we continue in these verses.

But a certain fearful looking for of judgment and fiery indignation, which shall devour the adversaries. This verse tells us of a coming judgement from God. The God of the bible as a loving God must be a God of judgement. A parent must judge and punish their child when they do wrong, so must God who loves us unconditionally punish us for our wrongdoing.

The lost only have the judgement in this verse to look forward to. I have said many times, without Christ the lost have no hope. All they have to look forward to is this fiery indignation that waits for them when they step into eternity. We as the children of God do not have this judgement to look forward to but we will receive judgement for our sins. Especially for the sins which we have not confessed.

The great thing about the God of the bible is that we can confess our sins to him, and he will forgive us from those sins and he will cleanse our hearts and wash them white as snow once we have repented of them. The genie god cannot forgive us from our sins. Since this genie god does not have the power to forgive us our sins, neither does he have the power to convict us from that sin. Therefore, the genie god who the worldly person thinks is in the bible, as long as he will remain in that closed bible collecting dust on our shelf, is the god that the world wants. They can open it when they are in need and close it when they are not. Like pulling the cork off the bottle, letting the genie out and then putting the cork back in the bottle and keeping the genie there until the next time he is needed.

This fiery indignation will devour all the lost. This verse is simply laying out the path for the lost who reject the God of the bible. The saved who reject the God of the bible are called Carnal. Carnal simply defined is: worldly. When reading the bible and you see the verse that talks about the carnal mind it is butitng heads with the God of the bible. This is carnality, it is worldliness. This verse is just simply talking about a future judgement that is coming. **Romans 14:12** says it best, **So then every one of us SHALL give an account of HIMSELF to God.** This included the saved as well as the lost. There is no need in the bible to dwell on the punishment for the hopeless lost. Their eternal destiny is set until they chose to accept Christ as their saviour. The bible is all about the chastisements, and punishments, which are the judgements form God for the saved.

Each and every person will at some point Havre to stand before God and answer for his choice. Will have to give an account of why we want the genie to serve us and not us to serve the God of the bible. Christians all I can say is it is a fearful thing to fall into the hands of a God that is alive and has all the power of Heaven and earth at his beckoning call.

He that despised Moses' law died without mercy under two or three witnesses: In Old Testament times when a child of God willfully sinned, they were confronted by the people and if that sin was not stopped, they were killed. They would be taken out in front of witnesses and stoned to death for their sin. This was a way to stop the rebellion. This was what they did because they loved and feared the God of the bible. The God of the bible will be a God that one will fear. I am not talking about being afraid of God himself. I am talking about fearing the chastisement from God that will make one think twice before he commits that sin, before he makes that willful choice.

The book of Proverbs is all about disciplining a child when they mess up. It is about warning that child not to hang out with certain friends, or go certain places, because those friends are likely to lead that person to sinful temptations. This is how we are to fear the God of the bible. We are to understand that judgement is coming whether you like it or agree with it, it is coming. We are to fear this coming judgement that we will want to do what the bible says to do. We will want to live for God so we can hear him say "well done" to us.

Of how much sorer punishment, suppose ye, shall he be thought worthy, who hath trodden under foot the Son of God, and hath counted the blood of the covenant, wherewith he was sanctified, an unholy thing, and hath done despite unto the Spirit of grace? The focus of this verse should be on the words "Thought worthy" this whole passage is talking about the lost soul who rejects God. I am also using the principle of those that reject God to the saved who reject what God says. There is a difference in the rejection of God which the lost soul has done, and the saved souls who has rejected what God says. I can love my parents, and I know they loves me, but I can reject what they say. When I do reject them, I suffer the consequences through chastisement.

In this verse we see that those who say they were children of God and truly were not, who understood the things of God but rejected them any way would have a sorer punishment. The Lost who reject God only reject God; those who know what God is about and reject him or what he says are held to a higher standard for punishment as they completely know what they were supposed to do. It is one thing to sin and not know you are sinning. It is a completely different things to know what that sin is and do it anyway.

The lost of this world will engage in acts of fornication, sometimes with many different partners. The lost of this world will enter into sinful legal marriages with persons of the same sex. The lost of this world will cheat, lie, and steal and not think twice about it. We ask why that is, because all the lost person knows is what their sin nature tells them. They do not know the things of God. They do not know what they are doing is sin. All they know about sin is if they are breaking a manmade law or not. Most of these people believe that they are overall good people. They do not understand the things of God and they do not understand that what they are doing is sin, all they know is that the sinful world tells them it is ok to do. Let's look at a verse to verify this. *I Corinthians 2:14 But the natural man receiveth not the things of the Spirit of God: for they are foolishness unto him: neither can he know them, because they are spiritually discerned*. In this verse it says that the things of the Spirit of God are FOOLISHNESS to him, and there is no way that he can

KNOW them because they are revealed to a person through the Holy Spirit. When a lost man remains lost, he knows nothing of the things of God, he wants nothing to do with the things of God. The only thing that the lost person can understand is the gospel. That why Jesus said in Matthew 28 to go into all the world and preach the gospel.

The saved person knows better, the saved person should never wat a genie god to serve them, they should want to serve the God of the bible. The saved person knowing better, is held to a higher standard of accountability than the lost. You may say well Pastor I thought there was no respect of persons with God, there is, you are correct, however the bible says in *James 4:17 Therefore to him that knoweth to do good, and doeth it not, to him it is sin.* Him that knoweth to do good is the saved. They have the Holy Spirit living inside of them, the things of God are revealed to them through the Holy Spirt yet when they chose to reject what the God of the bible says they are submitting to a genie god.

God holds his children to a higher standard than he does those that reject him when it comes to accountability. Look all through the bible, the bible tells us the lost are on their way to the lake of fire, that is it for them. For the saved however, the bible tells us that God takes the time to punish us and chastise us for our wrongdoing. God is patient with us during our rebellion, trying to chasten us enough to get us back to him. All the punishments for the lost are quick and final.

My fellow Christians if God holds us to a higher standard of accountability than he does the lost, then wouldn't it be smart to start to fear the living God of the bible and reject the genie god that the lost world craves for. We have gotten so far away from the things of God as Christians, we have stopped reading and believing our bibles, we are so focused on the things of the world like the lost are, all to what end, just to lose it all, just to be held accountable for our rejection of God's word. I lived like that for many years and I now refuse to live my life without God being first in it. I have learned the closer I get to God the less important the things of this world are to me. Yes, I had my genie god for many years, he served me well, only to the end of destruction in my life before I buried my genie god and turned to the living God.

For we know him that hath said, Vengeance belongeth unto me, I will recompense, saith the Lord. And again, The Lord shall judge his people. Recompense simply defined is: to return in kind. The Lord says that vengeance is his. He will judge the evil of this world. He will judge the sins that are not confessed, and he will judge his own people. Are you saved, then you are God's people? We as Christians are God's people, those in a carnal state, who rebel against what God says will suffer the condemnation that God brings upon a person he loves whom he is chastening.

We must go to **Romans 8:1** for a moment to prove my above statement. ***There is therefore now no condemnation to them which are in Christ Jesus, who walk not after the flesh, but after the Spirit.*** This verse says that one can be in Christ Jesus, which means they have been saved and are now a child of God, and if they do not walk after the flesh there will be no condemnation to them. There will be none of Gods judgement upon them. What about that saved Christian who is IN Christ Jesus, but choses to walk NOT after the Spirit, but after the flesh, the carnal Christian? They will suffer condemnation; they will suffer the judgement of God.

This verse in Hebrews is very clear that God will judge HIS people. He will not waste his time on the lost they are already condemned, lost without hope of ever reaching God without going through the shed blood of Jesus Christ. Don't let this world fool you, God's judgement is coming.

We as Christians are living like the God of the bible no longer exists. We live like there is no judgement. We live for our selfish desires and wants, and we have rejected the thigs of God. A carnal Christian will not read his bible and will not be on a path to seeking God. Oh, they will tell you they are, but they will not be. You can tell by the fruit in their lives. Statistics show that

47% of Christians, the saved, Children of God are addicted to Pornography. You cannot serve the God of the bible as your God if you are addicted to this trash. You are serving the genie god whom you only want to help you when you start to suffer the consequences of your sinful choices.

This is such a true statement, we all, when living in our sins, only call on God to help us when we begin to suffer the pain and anguish of OUR, not Gods, sinful choices. Most of us will take it a step further and blame God for allowing this to happen. We do this because we do not serve the God of the bible, we serve and only want the genie god because the genie god will not hold us accountable for our choice. The genie god will not convict our hearts when we are living in sin.

The soul that truly repents to God and accepts the consequences of his sinful choice, the soul that turns his ways back to God and starts to live for him is the soul that wants to serve the living God of the bible.

Out of that 47% of Christians that are addicted to pornography 50% are men and 20% are women. This is incredibly sad in today's society. Once we build a tolerance for this trash (SIN), we build a tolerance against the living God of the bible. We build a tolerance against the conviction of the Holy Spirit. Once a tolerance is built against the things of God, then sin is accepted in our lives, and the fruit of accepting sin, will be found in our homes, our churches, our jobs, and our society.

What are you teaching others around you? What are you teaching your children? Do they see you fearing the God of the bible or do they see you using a genie god to satisfy your sin? Believe it, don't believe it, that choice is yours. Just know that God's judgment is coming. It is coming for the lost, and for the carnal saved. You may not see his judgment here on this earth, there may be many of Gods people living in sin whom we don't see punishment come to them here on this earth, their judgement will be then in eternity. The bible says in **Hebrews 9:27 And as it is appointed unto men once to die, but after this the judgement:** did you see that? All will die, and after death is the judgement. Are you serving and fearing the living God of the bible, or are you happy with using your genie god to make you feel good while you are enjoying your sin?

You may be reading this and saying Pastor that is harsh, and yes, the truth is always harsh and difficult to hear. If we are only using a genie god, we are living in sin. We will see in the following chapters how Gods children, us the saved, have fallen into sin, how we love our sin, and we ridicule and persecute other bible believing Christians when they call out our sin. God will separate those who just say they love God from those that do love God. Or for the sake of this book, God will separate those of his children who are using a genie god, from those who are serving and fearing the living God of the bible.

It is a fearful thing to fall into the hands of the living God. The writer of the book of Hebrews is giving us, the children of God, a warning here in this verse. He is warning us that it will be a fearful thing for us to fall into God's judgement. It will not be pleasant for us to fall under the condemnation of God. When God chastens us, it is for our good. The bible says in ***Hebrews 12:6 For whom the Lord loveth he chasteneth, and scourgeth every son whom he receiveth.*** As children of God we are his sons, we are loved by him, we get chastened by him. Chastened simply defined is: to correct by punishment or suffering. God will allow us to go through the effects of our sins to get us back to him. This verse goes one step farther and says that not only does God chasten his children, but he also says that he will scourge EVERYONE he loves. Scourge simply defined is: a whip used to inflict pain. In other words, God will whip our butts for our wrongdoing.

I can remember many times in my life that my parents had to scourge me back into obedience as a child. We must understand that God is not a mean God, he is not a hateful God, he is a loving God. A loving God MUST punish sin and wrongdoing, and reward obedience. God had to punish the sin of Adam in the garden of Eden which effected all mankind, but through his grace, because of his love, he made a way for us to be back in that Holy state that we were originally created for.

Understanding that the God of the bible is a God of love, we must choose to serve him. We as Christians need to burry our genie god and get back to studying our bibles, get back to seeking FIRST the Kingdom of God, we need to get back to repentance and get forgiveness than and only then can God heal our land, can he heal our lives, and then and only then can we be free from the condemnation of God love upon us.

I lived serving a genie god for many years because he allowed me to be comfortable in my sin, he did not convict my heart of my sin, nor did he tell me what I need to do or how I needed to do it. My genie god let me live my life, the way I wanted to without consequences or judgement, and I was comfortable with this god. All was great until that day of condemnation came in my life, then my genie god had no power over the God of the bible whom I now serve and seek with all my heart and soul.

As we conclude this chapter and move on to the rest of the book you will see how we as Christians have replaced the God of the bible with the genie god. You will see how we have and still do enjoy our genie gods. Some will get mad at the rest of this book. I do want to challenge you that if you are one of those individuals that cannot handle opposite opinions or one of those that refuse to accept the truth of what will be said than please close this book and walk away. If what has been said so far has made you angry, I assure you that anger will not go away as you continue. If you bought this book, then send it back to me and I will refund your money.

It is not the intent of this book to incite anger, it is only to point out the truth of how the God of the bible has been replaced with the genie god we love. We will cover some topics that are near and dear to one's heart, such as patriotism, guns, gender identity, television, church, accreditations and many more topics. You must all through this book make a choice as to which God you will serve, but as for me and my house we will serve the Lord.

PATRIOTISM

Colossians 1:17 And he is before all things, and by him all things consist

It has been said by many good bible believing people that the United States of America was founded as a Christian nation. America as we know it today is in national crisis. Our constitution is being bent to the breaking point, twisted to the point of allowing some heinous sins to be legalized and churches and free speech to be pushed out, suppressed, and considered hate speech. The day is coming when the word of God will be considered hate speech and all who preach it will go to jail. This reality is approaching us fast.

Let's look at the founding of our country for a few minutes. When reading about the history of the United states we discover that this nation was not originally founded as a Christian nation. It was not founded on the word of God, nor was it founded on the God of the bible. The genie god was used to start this amazing nation. Before we continue, I must say that I am one hundred percent red-blooded American, I love this country and the freedoms it provides, I love that when the Christians were seeking God that God shed his grace on it. With that being said I am a child of God first and foremost. I place the bible higher than the constitution; I place biblical submission above my man-made freedoms, I adhere to the commands and principles of the bible at the cost of someday disobeying man-made laws when they go against the Word of God.

As I read the Declaration of Independence, which was the founding document for this great nation, I see that there are things in this document that do not line up with the God of the bible but do allow for a genie god to rule and reign.

The men of this time were men that originally rebelled against a God established government. Yes, God establishes governments not man. These men rebelled against a God ordained government because of man made money and man's desire to worship any god they chose to worship, in other words the want to worship a genie god and not the God of the bible.

Let's now look at a few verses that show that governments were and are established God. *1 Peter 3:22 Who is gone into heaven, and is on the right hand of God; angels and authorities and powers being made subject unto him.* This verse is talking about Jesus Christ. After Jesus rose from the grave on that third day he went to sit at the right hand of the father. He is still sitting there now, until the day that his Father God, tells him to go get his children.

This verse clearly says that all powers, all authorities, and all angels are subject to him, they are under the authority of Jesus Christ and not man. Subject simply defined is: one that is placed under authority. When man goes against the government, they in essence go against God with one exception. That exception being that when the government goes against the Word of God, or Bible established principles then one is to obey God rather than man. (Acts 5:29) God is not going to tell a person to go against a government he established for non-biblical issues like paying taxes, and the desire to have their genie god serve them. That would be a contradiction to his word. The bible tells us that the God of the bible is NOT the author of confusion. (I Corinthians 14:33)

Let's look at another passage in scripture. ***Romans 13:1-2 Let every soul be subject unto the higher powers. For there is no power but of God: the powers that be are ordained of God. Whosoever therefore resisteth the power, resisteth the ordinance of God: and they that resist shall receive to themselves damnation***. This passage says the same but with a punishment attached to it. Remember the bible is written for the saved, for God's children, it was not written for the lost who cannot understand the things of God.

This passage says there is NO, none, not of any kind, of government (Power) that is not ordained by God. This is the God of the bible. The God of the bible holds his people accountable for their actions, and their choices. If you have spent any time studying the life of Christ, you will not find one time where he went against the God ordained government. Even at his sham, made up lying trials he said nothing. He did not resist, he did not yell out, he obeyed God and submitted to those authorities.

There will be those reading this that say things like, we have the God given right to worship him, we have the right to assemble, and to that I will say yes to, and praise the Lord, but let me ask this question, what about the persecuted church in these godless countries, that have already ruled the bible as hate speech, these churches meet in underground bunkers, they meet in private homes, if it is a God given right to free assembly than why is the church that the Lord Jesus Christ established having to hide to meet? Because the right to free assembly in nowhere in the bible. It is in the bible that we are not to forsake the assembling of ourselves, it never says where that assembling has to take place. The bible gives no command to have a building for a church to meet in, it gives no command for the church to have open tent revivals. Yes, all these things are magnificent and should be used to reach the lost, but they are not commanded by God, they are freedoms granted by a man-made constitution that because of bible believing Christians who were seeking the God of the bible, God was shedding his grace on this great country.

The last part of this verse says that they that resist the God established power will bring damnation on themselves. Damnation simply defined is: judgement. When a person, saved or lost, goes against a government they risk damnation, judgement, to themselves. Just look at the state of the United States of America in the year 2020. It is a mess, it is in shambles, it is a nation that is divided. This nation was established to allow it to be divided, to allow it to be diverse, to allow all walks of life and all beliefs to be accepted. If you read your bibles, the bible tells us there is only ONE way to Heaven and that is thought he shed blood of Jesus Christ and that any and all other beliefs must be rejected. So, then I must ask, if there is only one way to Heaven, and all beliefs that differ from the bible must be rejected, then how can the USA be a

Christian nation when the founding Fathers, and the founding documents on this great nation are established against the Word of God? It cannot be. America was established to have a genie god to serve it, and not serve the God of the bible.

It is impossible for any nation, past, present, or future to be established as a Christian nation. Because most people reject the God or the Jesus Christ of the bible and have changed them into a genie, or a being that works for them. As long as there is lost people, there will never, ever, ever, be a Christian nation.

It is during oppression, and suppression that the Word of God, the gospel of Jesus Christ, is spread. It is during these times that the lost come to Christ. Yes, it is difficult for Christians to live in non-free countries, and most of the time they lose any and all personal belongings, but God tells us that from the beginning, that those who live godly in Christ will suffer persecution. (II Timothy 3:12). After all, look at the men of the bible, they all live in non-free countries, they were all living in persecution, and they all had no or very little earthly possessions.

The Beginning

We must now go to the founding of this great nation and look at some paragraphs from the founding documents and see how they line up with the bible. The following excerpt is from the Declaration of independence. (bold, italicized, and underlines have been added for emphasis)

In Congress, July 4, 1776

*The unanimous Declaration of the thirteen United States of America, When in the Course of human events, it becomes necessary for one people to dissolve the political bands which have connected them with another, and to assume among the powers of the earth, the separate and equal station to which **the Laws of Nature and of Nature's God entitle** them,*

 Even in our Declaration of Independence, Thomas Jefferson, who penned the document referred to some kind of a genie god. He used the phrase "Natures God" Nature's god is NOT the God of the bible. Almost everyone believes in some sort of god. Most religions have God at the base of it whether they deny the sonship of Jesus Christ or not.

Thomas Jefferson himself did not believe that Jesus was the only way to go to Heaven. He denied that Jesus was THE son of God but A son of God. When one denies that Jesus is the son of God, they deny the bible. The bible says there is only ONE way to Heaven and that is through the shed blood of Jesus Christ.

If you noticed in the paragraph, the document does not say that God gave them the right to be a free nation. It does not say that they are required to be a free people. It does not say that to live for God one must be free, no it says that natures god has ENTITLED them to be a separate people.

The God of the bible was never put into this document. To say the United States was a Christian nation, or that it was founded upon Christian principles is not the truth. As we see so far it was founded by men who rebelled against God by going against a God-ordained, already established government, to form another government that never included the God of the bible into it. It has reference to their form of a genie god but not the God of the bible. Just to make this point clear any genie god is a god of Satan. If it is not the God of the bible, it is then the god of Satan. Remember in the Ten Commandment the words of the Lord, ***Exodus 20:3 Thou shalt have no other gods before me.*** This was the very first commandment God placed to the children of Israel. We now have the greatest country on the face of this earth for this time period, who has placed their genie god, natures god, ahead of the God of the bible.

One may ask as I have, if this country was not founded on God, or on biblical principles, then why has it been so blessed? That is a great question, and the answer to that is simple. There are true Christians in this country who are seeking the God of the bible. There are Christians who are praying for this nation and God is hearing their prayers. We see in II Chronicles 7:14 that if God's people are seeking him and are getting rid of the sins in their lives, then God heals and restores their nations.

The thing we in America today have to be concerned with is that we as Christians are no longer fighting against sin, we are cleaving to our sins. We have placed our genie gods before the God of the bible, and he is mad at that. Look at the events in the bible in the book of Revelation, when the tribulation period comes, why is all the evil running rampant, is because there are no more Christians there praying for God to heal the land. They have been raptured out at that time. If there are none of Gods people there, he withdraws his hand on that nation. God will also allow a nation to be in distress for his people, not the lost, because of the sins they have embraced. It has been said that Satan is no longer fighting against the church, he has now started to join the church. Such a true statement.

The simple solution is that we as the saved children of the God of the bible, have to repent of our sins, and turn from our wicked ways so God can heal our land. We can place all the people we want into government offices; we can fight all the abortion clinics in the world, we can march against all the homosexual movements ever planned, but if we do not get the sin out of OUR own personal lives and repent that change will never come. Remember the verse in **Hebrews 10:31 It is a <u>FEARFUL</u> thing to fall into the hands of the <u>LIVING GOD.</u>** We as Christians must take heed to this verse. If we keep cleaving to our genie god and keep making him first in our lives and placing him above the God of the bible there will be consequences to pay. We are already seeing this in our nation as we speak.

 We do have certain right according to the bible. Right simply defined is: acting or judging in accordance with truth. To understand these right that are in our declaration of independence we must go to the bible.

The first one is the right to life, the bible tells us in the book of Psalms that we are made by God, He knew every part of us before we were formed, yes, we have the right to life. *Psalm 139:13-16 For thou hast possessed my reins: thou hast covered me in my mother's womb. I will praise thee; for I am fearfully and wonderfully made: marvellous are thy works; and that my soul knoweth right well. My substance was not hid from thee, when I was made in secret, and curiously wrought in the lowest parts of the earth. Thine eyes did see my substance, yet being unperfect; and in thy book all my members were written, which in continuance were fashioned, when as yet there was none of them.*

The question is now, does it matter what country you were born in, does it matter if you know what time area you were born in, NO. people in the bible were born, raised, lived, and served the God of the bible with all forms of governments at hand. Most of which were oppressive, communistic cultures. Most of which killed Christians for what they believed. Does the bible tell us to only serve God when we are free to do so, NO! the bible tells us to go into the world and tell others about

Jesus, period. The bible tells us NOT to lay up treasures in the earth but to lay up treasures in Heaven. That is our right to life is to live for God. God promises that HE will meet ALL our needs all we have to do is trust him, yet we refuse to do so.

The next one was the right to liberty. Liberty simply defined is: Freedom. Yes, God gave each and every one of us a freewill to make our own choices, to live our lives the way we want to live them but we as Christians through the power of the Holy Spirit have a God given liberty from sin, not from oppressive governments, not from laws which man has established, as Christians the liberty we have is the liberty to serve God. The Holy Spirit gives us the power over our sin, to live for God. This liberty has not one thing to do with any kind of a man manded liberty. It is the liberty one has in Christ once they have accepted his gift of salvation. This passage says it all about the right of liberty that a Christian has. ***Romans 8:1-4 There is therefore now no condemnation to them which are in Christ Jesus, who walk not after the flesh, but after the Spirit. <u>For the law of the Spirit of life in Christ Jesus hath made me free from the law of sin and death</u>. For what the law could not do, in that it was weak through the flesh, God sending his own Son in the likeness of sinful flesh, and for sin, condemned sin in the flesh: <u>That the righteousness of the law might be fulfilled in us, who walk not after the flesh, but after the Spirit.</u>*** If you study the underlined parts of this passage, you will see that the liberty that the Christian has is to fulfill the righteousness of the law of Christ, in other words we have the liberty to serve God as we are freed from the bondage of sins death.

The last one in this section is the right to the "pursuit of happiness" this section should be an eye opener for the saved person reading this. This is more proof that we as Christians have turned TO our wicked ways and have a genie god serving us and have placed this god before the God of the bible. If you look up the word happy in the bible you will see it is all about doing it God's way. If you live for him, you will be happy, if you live for him, you will be persecuted, and maybe even kilt, but you will be happy to suffer for him. Our pursuit of happiness is simply to suffer for Christ by living for him and seeking him with all our hearts, minds, and souls. It is not about feeling good in this sinful world, it is not about feeling good in a god-less society. Lets go to the bible.

James 5:11Behold, we count them <u>happy</u> which endure. Ye have heard of the patience of Job, and have seen the end of the Lord; that the Lord is very pitiful, and of tender mercy. There are a couple of verses in the bible that tell us about the pursuit of happiness. The biblical pursuit of happiness starts the moment one accepts Jesus Christ as their Saviour. Once they begin to seek him, they find a happiness that only comes through Jesus. This happiness will be there in the best times of one's life, and the worst times of one's life. This happiness is associated with peace.

The happiness that is found in Jesus is true happiness, this happiness also comes in the form of painful suffering and persecution for the cause of Jesus Christ.

The United States has no idea whatsoever what persecution is all about. The constitution grants them freedom from that persecution. The bible tells us in **II Timothy 3:12, Yea and all that will live godly in Christ Jesus, <u>SHALL</u> suffer persecution.** Did you see that? they shall suffer! If one is not being persecuted for Christ, then they have no idea how well their faith will stand the test. The United states has loved this genie god they have created, this genie god makes them feel good, it protects them from suffering, it allows diversity in all faiths, we will discuss more on this in a few minutes. This genie god is what this country loves and puts all their heart and money and souls into. Over the years good bible believing churches have stood against this genie god, but today even the churches have welcomed it in with wide open arms. People just don't believe the bible. And Christians don't believe it enough to change their lives.

One thing I will say about the United states is this is the only country in the world that has bibles at in abundance. Most of the time you can find one somewhere or someone will give you one. We have such access to the Holy word of God and yet we reject it. It is a fearful thing to fall into the hands of the living God.

1 Peter 3:14 But and if ye suffer for righteousness' sake, <u>happy</u> are ye: and be not afraid of their terror, neither be troubled; We see hear that in biblical happiness that there could be terror associated with it.

When a person is walking with God, they are so protected from the evil of the world spiritually, that all of man's efforts cannot make one afraid.

If one suffers for the cause of Christ, (righteousness sake) they will experience an intimacy with Christ like never experienced before. This is true happiness. This is the happiness that the God of the bible brings to one that is seeking him. This Godly happiness gives you peace in the midst of the wort time in your life knowing that Jesus is right there with you step by step.

1 Peter 4:13-14 But rejoice, inasmuch as ye are partakers of Christ's sufferings; that, when his glory shall be revealed, ye may be glad also with exceeding joy. If ye be reproached for the name of Christ, happy are ye; for the spirit of glory and of God resteth upon you: on their part he is evil spoken of, but on your part he is glorified. Godly happiness is not our surface happiness here in this godless world. Our happiness as Christians is found when the glory of Jesus Christ is revealed. This glory gets revealed for us that are saved at our death the moment we enter into eternity, or at the blessed hope of the catching away of the saved that are still alive. The glory of Jesus will be revealed to the world at the end of the tribulation period when Jesus Christ returns not as a lamb led to the slaughter, but he returns as the king of kings, and the Lord of Lords. This life in this world is only but a drop in the bucket compared to eternity.

The last part of this verse says that when people cause you to suffer for Christ that on their end, they will speak evil of you, they will lie, they will abuse, they will do anything in their power to destroy you because they hate the message of Jesus Christ. For the Christian who rejoices in this suffering, and resists the fighting back allows God to be glorified. Jesus set the example for us, he never said a word, he never fought back, he never reacted inappropriately, he was in today's world considered a wimp or a sissy. He did this because he knows that once this sacrifice is made, once his blood is shed, he is declared not just a king, but the King of Kings and the LORD of lords. This goes for us as Christians, we may suffer for the cause of Christ, but our happiness is knowing that we are the children of the God of the bible, and once this life here is over, we will rule and reign along with Jesus Christ. What a great hope that is for us.

This happiness is not produced by the United States genie god that this founding document was trying to make people think it was. We have such a mis construed idea that the United States is a Christian nation, and that God blesses it because of that. The genie god does not allow for the God of the bible to have access to this nation in its founding. The only reason that this great nation has been blessed as I said before is because of the God-seeking Christians praying for this country and spreading the gospel. The pursuit of happiness in the Declaration of

Independence is only a fairy tale told by a genie god who is under the control of Satan. You can have the biblical pursuit of happiness by starting to seek God with all your heart, all your mind, and all your soul.

 I find it very interesting that in the Declaration of Independence that is says that it is right of the people to alter or abolish governments. If we compare the Declaration of Independence to the bible it says this, yes, the God of the bible established the government, but I don't like this government so I will rub my little bottle and my genie god will come out and let me make a new government regardless of what the God of the bible thinks or says. This is it in a nutshell.

How was the United States founded as a Christian nation? This is truly Nature's god that this is built on, Nature's god is a genie god under the control of Satan himself. Like others I enjoy the freedoms that this country has. This is not about our freedoms, or even having any notion that the United States is an evil country, this is about Gods Children, worshiping and serving a genie god that makes them feel good, and rejecting the God of the bible.

We see again that this nation believes it is their right to overthrow a God ordained government, for their own selfish pride and comfort. We all want our families to live in peace, I get that, I want that for my family as well. The bible tells us as Christians that we are to live peacefully in this world, we are Not to get involved in Seditions, Uprisings against the governments (Galatians 5:19-20)

Some who read this will get very angry with what I say here. That is ok, I have big shoulders, just bring your complaints to me from the Word of God and not your hurt pride. Christians have no business in uprisings against governments. We have no business in resisting laws and mandates instituted by our governmental officials, unless those laws and mandates tell us to do something against the Word of God then we are to find joy in suffering the consequences of that resistance. If the governments, and ruling powers are ordained by the God of the bible than don't you think that that same God of the bible will judge those governments and establish and new governments if they will. The reason why Gods children worship the genie god and place him higher that the God of the bible is because they refuse to repent of their sins, and to turn from their wicked ways. Once the cork is placed on the bottle with the genie god living in it and that bottle is buried never to be found again, then the God of the bible can heal any and all lands that seek him. It is not till then. Remember it is a FEARFUL thing to fall not the hands of the LIVING GOD. (Hebrews 10:31)

THE CONSTITUTION

This will be a section that may upset a lot of good bible believing Christians as that is not the intent of this section. The Constitution of the United States of America is an amazing document. Most governments are based on dictatorship rule, where we are based on a document rule. I will offer a fact of reality that this document is only as good as the people supporting it.

We have seen here in the year 2020 that this document has been pushed to the limit and depending on the outcome of this year's election it will be pushed to breaking point, or even possibly destroyed. God has not, let me repeat that, God has NOT called Christians to make defending a constitution of a government that he establishes and removes more important the pages of the Holy Bible.

We have been so distracted by this constitution that we as bible believing Christians will spend, hours, days, weeks, and all our fortunes and give our lives to defend this document, while at the same time we get upset because we have to spend an hour or so in church on Sunday, we refuse to give to the local church and missions, and we would not be caught dead at our workplaces professing Jesus Christ as our Lord and Saviour. Our bibles lay on our shelves collecting dust while our TVs become our new basis of right or wrong. Again, I am not trying to offend anyone just pointing out reality. The genie god of this world has become the god that almost everyone worships. I worshiped him myself for many years. It wasn't until I put that genie back in the bottle and made the God of the bible my intention that my life started to change.

The United States Constitution is like no other document. It has been said that this document is from God and it provides "God-given rights" this is what we must examine. As with the Declaration of Independence, we must compare it to the bible to see if our rights are truly God-given or are they just God-allowed as a blessing for seeking him.

The basis of this country was not founded on God as we discussed in the last section, however God has shed his grace on this great nation because of bible believing Christians who are seeking him with all their hearts, minds, and souls. Make sure you completely understand this one thing, it is Christians seeking God that has allowed his grace on this country, not a piece of paper with the word constitution on it. When Christians start to remove the God of the bible and replace him with a genie god, this once great nation will start to fall as we are witnessing today.

Let's look at a couple of verses in the bible that prove my statement above. *2 Chronicles 7:14-15 If my people, which are called by my name, shall humble themselves, and pray, and seek my face, and turn from their wicked ways; then will I hear from heaven, and will forgive their sin, and will heal their land. Now mine eyes shall be open, and mine ears attent unto the prayer that is made in this place. 2 Chronicles 7:14-15 If my people, which are called by my name,* who are God's people, Who are called by HIS name? us bible believing Christians. The bible was written well before the constitution was even a thought in man's eye. *shall humble themselves, and pray, and seek my face, and turn from their wicked ways;* God's people, followed by being intentional, in seeking him, in turning from their wicked ways; worshiping, or even longing for a genie god is a wicked way. Most, not all, most Christians today only want the genie god because they enjoy their sins too much. They enjoy the pleasures of this world for the moment and choose to ignore the eternal rewards that the God of the bible gives.

In life everything has a price. When it comes to serving God there is also a price to be paid. If one chooses to serve God, it will cost them popularity with the world. If one, choose to serve God they die to themselves. When one chooses to serve God, they do it usually with no security or even pleasure. Those who chose to serve the God of the bible will have a joy in their hearts that only God can bring about, but the temporary pleasures of this world will not be desired. When one chooses to serve their genie god, it will be at the cost of the God of the bible.

Do you sit around sometimes and wonder why this nation is in the distress that it is in? it is because the God of the bible has been replaced with our genie god and sin has been accepted. It has been accepted in our churches even to the point of allowing ungodly people to be pastors and church leaders, woe unto them that change the truth of God into a lie. We as Christians have followed suit to this sin, we have grown callous to sin and have accepted it as normal. If you don't believe me walk into just about any church and you will hear tolerance, acceptance of all, you will see Christians with bumper stickers that say God is love, and we all need to coexist. This is what the genie god produces. The God of the bible says that sin is sin, that there is punishment for our sins, and that God will judge a person based on those sins. Woe to you hypocrites, who defile the name of God and call yourselves Christians while worshipping a genie god. Remember it is a FEARFUL thing to fall into the hands of a living God, the God of the bible.

then will I hear from heaven, and will forgive their sin, and will heal their land. As Gods people turn from their sins, as they put their genies back into their bottles, they will begin to turn back to the God of the bible. Because God does love us, he will hear our land.

He will destroy the evil; he will get his will accomplished.

As you study your bibles you will see that Gods people have a history that repeats itself time and time again, as we are experiencing today. There are times in biblical history that Gods people would seek him, would love him, would worship him, and would serve him. Their nation was at peace, their lives were blessed, and God was providing their needs. They were happy, they were satisfied, and they had the joy of the Lord in abundance on them. Then after a few generations they began to disobey God, their nation became at war, their peace was taken away. As they continue to drift from the God of the bible, they began to get into more and more oppression. To the points of being in captivity. They would uncork the bottles and ask their genie for their three wishes, and while at times for small things they may have gotten what they asked for, but it was temporary. It was not until God's people had lost everything, that they realized that the genie god was controlled by Satan. It was then they would turn back to the God of the bible for healing.

This continued all through biblical and worldly history. It is happening today as I write this book. Our lives are not at peace, our nation is at war. Our nation is at war amongst itself. Many lives have been wasted, many have been lost all due to rebellion against the God of the bible and a desire for the genie who can't do anything for them. Unlike the bible times, we have the complete word of God at our disposal, we have the answers to ALL our issues, but our genie has gotten us so focused on him that we would rather lose everything we have, we would sacrifice even our very God given lives to protect a document that allows us to reject the God of the bible and we wonder why our nation is in distress.

Now mine eyes shall be open, and mine ears attent unto the prayer that is made in this place. Once Gods people start to realize that their genie god is a puppet of Satan and they turn back to the God of the bible, the living God, then they have his full attention. Then he can begin to heal their nation, then we can begin to see souls saved and lives changed for his glory. We can put in office all the Christian men we want into our leadership roles, we can have all the freedom this ungodly world can offer but until God's people, turn from their wicked ways our nation will continue on the path of destruction, to the point it no longer exists. And that my friend is fact. It is not the lost of this world destroying our nation, it is us, who have replaced the God of the bible, with our genie god.

As we examine the constitution of this great nation, we see that it establishes a form of governmental operations. It has detailed outlines for how our government is to operate, how procedures are to happen, and how power and authority are established or removed. It almost sounds like the instructions that we have in the Word of God.

In our constitution we have the bill of rights, also known as our amendments. These are foundational laws of this constitution that grant each person the same rights (freedoms) to live by. Though we will not discuss all these amendments, we will discuss the first two amendments as they seem to be the focus of almost all Christians in the nation today. These have become the focus so much that they have caused good Christian men and women to sacrifice their relationships with the God of the bible and become married to their genie gods.

THE Conventions of a number of the States, having at the time of their adopting the Constitution, expressed a desire, in order to prevent misconstruction or abuse of its powers, that further declaratory and restrictive clauses should be added: And as extending the ground of public confidence in the Government, will best ensure the beneficent ends of its institution. The first clause of the constitution allows for the people of the nation to have confidence in themselves. It allows them to have a more pleasant life. It allows them to be free from abuse. I do not see anywhere in this document encouraging people to seek the God of the bible for their security. I do not see where it tells people to go to their bibles and get involved in the biblical church. It is all about promoting selfishness in a god-less society. When this nation or any nation is NOT built on the bible or has a focus on the God of the bible, they will cling to their genie god.

We will go to the bible for some reminders about putting a genie god before the living God. **Deuteronomy 4:23-24**

Take heed unto yourselves, lest ye forget the covenant of the Lord your God, which he made with you, this is a clear warning about drifting your focus from the God of the bible. The bible is very clear that God's children are to focus and live for Him not for things of this world that will all be destroyed in the end.

Living Gods way has eternal rewards which can never be destroyed. These eternal rewards when you leave this earth will still be with you. When you focus on the worldly things made by sinful men not a single thing can you take with you when you leave this world.

and make you a graven image, or the likeness of anything, which the Lord thy God hath forbidden thee. Did you see that? Or the LIKENESS of anything which the Lord forbids. When a person or in this case a nation is based on their own self pleasure, their own self security, and living by sight and not by faith they are building their life and nation on sin and not the solid rock of God. Romans 14:23 tells us that whatever we do if it is not built on faith it is sin.

The United States is a great nation, I love living in this freedom that God has granted us, with that being said, it was built on ungodly standards, from ungodly men seeking their own self-satisfaction. And that my friend, one day will fail. If it is not built on God, it will fail. We as Christians, God's children have drifted to this self-satisfying mind set ourselves and that is why this nation is in distress because we have turned from the God of the bible to the genie god.

For the Lord thy God is a consuming fire, even a jealous God. God makes the statement that he is a consuming fire which simply means this. If we don't turn from our sinful ways, the God of the bible will destroy the genie god we love so much to get our attention so we can start to serve the God of the bible again. I want to challenge you to get your eyes back on the God of the bible, kill your genie god, if you don't God will.

RESOLVED by the Senate and House of Representatives of the United States of America, in Congress assembled, two thirds of both Houses concurring, that the following Articles be proposed to the Legislatures of the several States, as amendments to the Constitution of the United States, all, or any of which Articles, when ratified by three fourths of the said Legislatures, to be valid to all intents and purposes, as part of the said Constitution;

ARTICLES in addition to, and Amendment of the Constitution of the United States of America, proposed by Congress, and ratified by the Legislatures of the several States, pursuant to the fifth Article of the original Constitution.

Note: The following text is a transcription of the first ten amendments to the Constitution in their original form. These amendments were ratified December 15, 1791, and form what is known as the "Bill of Rights."

The First Amendment

AMENDMENT I

Congress shall make no law respecting an establishment of religion, or prohibiting the free exercise thereof; this first sentence of the first amendment of the constitution is what all churches in the United States value more than life itself. That is the freedom of worship. This is such an amazing amendment and has led to the freedom of religious exercise for many years. It has led many bible believing Christians and churches into courts to protect this right.

When we get to the base of this amendment it is not an amendment to promote serving the God of the bible, it is a man-made protection for people to worship and serve their genie god. It is simply an amendment to condone sinful activity and have it protected. As your blood is now boiling that a bible believing pastor has made such a heinous statement about your right to worship let's see what this amendment really says and then compare it to the bible.

An establishment of religion simply allows ANY AND ALL beliefs to have a church. It allows for ANY AND ALL false doctrines to reside in the hearts of Gods people. Here where I currently live in Colorado which at the time of this writing is a legal Marijuana state. This "Establishment of RELIGION" also allows this ungodly marijuana group to form a "religion" that is now protected as well. This group has in their services, smoking, drinking and drugs as they claim that is what their religion believes. So, I must ask, would the God of the bible allow such gross sin to be classified with his word? Would he allow such sinful activity to be promoted among the people to who he created? What about the Satanists who have their own religion, our first amendment allows for them to worship freely as well? Does the God of the bible support Satan worship? NO he does not. This is an amendment that protects and promotes the satanic genie god of this world that so many of us have clung to, even to the point of sacrificing everything to protect this ungodly amendment.

We as God's children have used this amendment to promote the things of God. We have used this to get the gospel out, but we can do that even under oppression. How many apostles, prophets, and men of God in the bible had this right, not a one of them. Yet the gospel still flourished, many souls got saved, and there was truly a nation of revival, this was simply because they worshiped the God of the bible and fought to destroy the genie god of Satan. Yet our founding fathers made a way to promote the genie god which many of us love.

I am not saying I do not support the first amendment, I am simply saying that God cannot and will not be in support of a law that allows ungodly, unbiblical idol worship to be classified with him and his word, here is what the bible says about this.

2 Corinthians 6:14-18 Be ye not unequally yoked together with unbelievers: for what fellowship hath righteousness with unrighteousness? and what communion hath light with darkness? This is very clear. The God of the bible and Satan CANNOT in any way be associated with each other yet we as God's children will sacrifice everything we have just to rebel against this passage and support ALL RELIGIONS to have the same protections.

If I were to ask any bible believing Christian if it would be sin to promote Satan, and the things of Satan, every one of them would overwhelmingly say yes. But those exact same Christians will support the Satanists in their right to have a church or a religion that decimates the things of God by fighting for the protection of the first amendment of the constitution.

And what concord hath Christ with Belial? or what part hath he that believeth with an infidel? And what agreement hath the temple of God with idols? What agreement hath the things of God with the things of the world. NOT ONE SINGLE THING. We spend so much time, money, and effort fighting for something that God says is sin while sacrificing lost souls on their way to a burning Hell. Remember this simple truth, you cannot stand in the protest line to protect your first amendment right without the Satanists, the Islamicist, Catholics, and who ever standing right there with you. You cannot protect your first amendment right to worship without protecting theirs as well. What AGREEMENT hath the things of God with idols? NONE. This is something that the genie god allows and not the God of the bible.

for ye are the temple of the living God; as God hath said, I will dwell in them, and walk in them; and I will be their God, and they shall be my people. The God of the bible is all the right to worship we need. The God of the bible is all the "religious freedom" we can have. If we serve the God of the bible, he and only he will make a way for us to get the gospel message out. The bible tells us plainly that *...**all that will live godly in Christ Jesus SHALL suffer persecution II Timothy 3:12*** if we live godly, we will not be protecting our right to worship which allows the genie god the same right, we will suffer persecution for the message in which we bring. But we will still preach the word.

Wherefore come out from among them, and be ye separate, saith the Lord, and touch not the unclean thing; and I will receive you, And will be a Father unto you, and ye shall be my sons and daughters, saith the Lord Almighty. Simply put, we are to be SEPARATE from the things of Satan, separate from the things of this sinful world, yes, my friends, who are still reading this, we are not to support anything that forces us to unite with Satan and his army, as the first amendment forces us to do.

or abridging the freedom of speech, or of the press; or the right of the people peaceably to assemble, and to petition the Government for a redress of grievances.

The Second Amendment

AMENDMENT II

A well regulated Militia, being necessary to the security of a free State, the right of the people to keep and bear Arms, shall not be infringed.
Militia simply defined is: a group of people that defend individual rights against government oppression. The second amendment was an amendment designed for the citizens of the United States to be able to defend themselves against evil and against an oppressive government. The Constitutions was designed for the government to work for the people not the people to work for the government. This was a great thing for many years.

In recent years this right has been infringed upon. There have been laws put in place trying to limit people from having guns, have delayed the purchases of guns, and have taxed very highly the purchase of guns. Guns since their invention will always be around. Once the laws get more enforced, and guns become more illegal to have the more illegal guns will be out there.

I have heard many bible believing Christians claim that they will die defending their right to carry their guns. This is well and good as for any right to be protected it must be defended. I am not saying I believe in not fighting for our rights, I am saying that we must be very sure that as Christians when we are fighting to defend out right to bear arms that we are not sacrificing our right to carry our bibles.

Almost every bible believing Christian I know will stand for hours upon hours to defend their right to bear arms. These same Christians will, if pushed to, stand and fight against all opposition for this right. At the same time when the principles are kicking bibles and God out of our schools. They are not standing and fighting against that. Their mind set is man that's not right, they might even say a prayer for that situation then they go about their lives saying how evil and wicked the public-school systems are. I do agree that if you put your Children in an ungodly school system, they will get trained by god hating people.

My point is simply this, we as Christians will spend hours, days, fortunes, to defend our right to carry our guns but will overall remain silent for our right to carry our bibles. We have learned to worship our genie god while blaming the God of the bible when things go wrong. I said blaming the God of the bible. It is so easy for us as Christians to serve our genie god that makes us so focused on ourselves and our rights to keep our comforts so we can continue to live our selfish lives. Then when all falls apart, we want to blame the God of the bible for allowing this to happen when it was us that made those stupid choices.

How many Christian parents have trained their children in this same pattern? How many of us as parents have taught our children that the right to bear arms is far greater that our right to carry our bibles. You say Pastor that is ridiculous, I ask you then, what have they seen you defend more, the right to carry your gun, or the right to carry your bible? Children see what their parents do. Are you in those second amendment marches on Washington, or are you in those Saturday night prayer meeting for lost souls to come to Jesus?

When I was growing up, I went to our church school, we had a gun range out back, and we were allowed gun club as an elective. That was awesome. Men in the church would have the Sheriff's department show up for competition shootings. These events are well and good.

Everyone would enjoy themselves. And many men and families would show up to watch.

The next Sunday in church the Pastor would tell people that on Thursday night was visitation to go see people that were out of church, or had just visited, and no one would show up. Why was that, because these same bible believing Christians that spend hours, and resources to do what they enjoy, refuse to sacrifice their time and efforts for the God of the bible. Their first love is their genie god and not the God of the bible.

We now will go to the Bile to see what God has to say about putting our second amendment before him. *Revelation 2:1-5 Unto the angel of the church of Ephesus write; These things saith he that holdeth the seven stars in his right hand, who walketh in the midst of the seven golden candlesticks; I know thy works, and thy labour, and thy patience, and how thou canst not bear them which are evil: and thou hast tried them which say they are apostles, and are not, and hast found them liars: And hast borne, and hast patience, and for my name's sake hast laboured, and hast not fainted. Nevertheless I have somewhat against thee, because thou hast left thy first love. Remember therefore from whence thou art fallen, and repent, and do the first works; or else I will come unto thee quickly, and will remove thy candlestick out of his place, except thou repent.*

Revelation 2:1-5 Unto the angel of the church of Ephesus write; These things saith he that holdeth the seven stars in his right hand, who walketh in the midst of the seven golden candlesticks; I know thy works, and thy labour, and thy patience, and how thou canst not bear them which are evil: and thou hast tried them which say they are apostles, and are not, and hast found them liars: And hast borne, and hast patience, and for my name's sake hast laboured, and hast not fainted. Jesus points out here that this church was overall doing things in the spiritual realm that were the right things to do. They were rebuking the false prophets; they were working and laboring in love for Christ. They were doing the actions of the church, but they had lost something in the process. One can get so busy in the things of God that they begin to lose focus on the cross and the meaning of the gospel of Jesus Christ.

Jesus clearly points this out to them. In today's church the children of God are not even doing the actions of the church. They are not even living the life pleasing to God. They are living so far in the world that they cannot be known as Christians. Like with his church in Ephesus, they have the outward actions that serve a genie god to impress the God of the bible while their hearts are so far away from the things of the God of the bible that his work is being neglected, lost souls are going to Hell, and Christians actions are showing more people the broad way to destruction than the narrow way to Christ. I am not saying that supporting our second amendment right send people to Hell, I am saying that when we as God's children make the second amendment more of a focus than camp meetings, bible studies, revivals, prayer meetings, and witnessing, then we have lost our first love.

Nevertheless I have somewhat against thee, because thou hast left thy first love. Jesus says that he has an issue with this church. This issue is that everything they were doing they took their eyes off of Him and placed it on the world and the things of the world. I have been there. Even today it is easy to get distracted form the things of God as the issues of the world face us all the time.

Remember therefore from whence thou art fallen, and repent, and do the first works; or else I will come unto thee quickly, and will remove thy candlestick out of his place, except thou repent. Jesus gives a direct warning here he says for his children to REPENT. Repent is to simply turn back to God. The God of the bible not a genie god that always makes you feel good. Then Jesus goes into one more warning, he says that if this church, his church, does not repent he will remove their candlestick from them. In other words, he will remove his blessings form this church. He will let the consequences of the sinful directions they are heading start to take over. We see that today in our so-called "Christian Nation" that God's children have taken their eyes off of him and placed them on the world, and the candlestick has been removed from its place. It is a FEARFUL thing to fall into the hands of the living God.

Let me leave you with one last thought, if the first and second amendments were removed from this country, would the work of the Lord have to stop? No, it is commanded for us to preach the Gospel, there are no conditions to serving God, we are to serve, it don't matter if we are a free nation or an oppressed nation. What about the Christians in these communist nations that are being beaten, beheaded, and thrown in prison? They have no first or second amendment rights they are still getting the gospel out. We are seeing souls come to Jesus in these countries by the thousands because they are focused on their first love. America is soon to be no longer a free nation unless God's people begin to bury their genie god of self service and start to serve the God of the bible with self-sacrifice. The greater reward that is eternal is the self-sacrificing service to the God of the bible.

TREASURE

Matthew 6:19-21 Lay not up for yourselves treasures upon earth, where moth and rust doth corrupt, and where thieves break through and steal: But lay up for yourselves treasures in heaven, where neither moth nor rust doth corrupt, and where thieves do not break through nor steal: For where your treasure is, there will your heart be also.

We live in a time where our focus has shifted to the things of this world. We have set our sights on having more and more.

We want things now and won't wait to get things. This has caused much debt in our society today. I have experienced this myself. I have a tendency to not wait for what I want or certain things. I guess you can say when it comes to material possessions I live for the moment.

Personally, I have never been one to put value in "things" of this world. I have never had to have the nice or the best of things. I have had many cars, houses, clothes shoes over the years, and to their end they all have for me, never filled a void. During my prodigal years I still never valued things. I really never had a desire to have lots of money, huge bank accounts, or retirement plans. I just got the stuff I needed for now, and worried about tomorrow when it came.

I still have that tendency to be like that but for me it is different now as I place absolutely no value on things whatsoever. I make my car payment not to have a nice car, but because for such a time as this I am driving a reliable car and my wife has a car that won't break down on her. So, if that means I make a monthly payment then so be it.

As I have learned to draw closer to God this verse becomes more of a reality to me. ***Philippians 4:19 But my God shall supply all your need according to his riches in glory by Christ Jesus***. We will discuss this verse in detail before this chapter is over.

My wife and I frequent estate sales. These are different from your typical yard sales as an estate sale is a sale of people's stuff they have bought, and collected over the years and sometimes a lifetime it is an accumulation of everything they own. We, like many others, go to these sales and you can determine what kind of people they were, see what kind of books they read, and sort of know their history, while at the same time purchasing all their stuff for pennies on the dollar. I use this example to show that no matter how hard one works, how determined they were to get their stuff, how many hours of overtime, how much time was sacrificed with their family all this stuff was left behind to deteriorate or be fought over when they left this life here on earth. Not one single earthly thing they sacrificed for, not one, was able to go on to eternity with them, or after them. Only the things you do for Christ will be your reward.

When a person is walking with God they care less and less about what they have. They only care about the things of God and trusting him to provide. The God of the bible provides ALL our need if we let him, and not only does he provide our need he provides that need according to his riches in Glory. What does that mean? It simply means that the God of the bible owns everything, in Heaven and in earth. Since he owns everything in Heaven and in earth, he is capable of providing your individual using any and all resources. Which in simple terms says that you may have a need of one hundred dollars, he is capable of meeting that need with one hundred thousand dollars if you are seeking Him.

The genie god of this world who as a reminder is controlled by Satan, will tell you that you and you alone must meet your own need. That you must quit that job that allows you to focus on family and ministry, to get a job that pays more at the sacrifice of these two things to keep stuff that is impossible to take with you. To make this clearer the God of the bible wants your top focus on him and eternal rewards and let him provide your need, whereas the genie god of the world wants you to focus on your immediate needs on earth which are temporary. and have no eternal rewards in Heaven. I challenge you to talk to any rich person, or any person that is only focused on the things of this world and you will find as they recall their history that these things were never enough. These earthly things were for a moment then they wanted the newest version. It is impossible for sinful, worldly, earthly, things to satisfy and eternal appetite.

Every bible believing Christian should acquire this eternal appetite. If one is seeking the God of the bible that appetite will be the only appetite they desire. If one is drifting from the things of the God of the bible, they will develop that appetite for the things of this world. Oh, how this genie god of the world has manipulated God's people so much that they have gone down a Godless sinful path.

Christians today will take jobs that cause them to miss church, it will cost them their families, and they will be miserable in their lives. The main trick that this genie god uses is he makes one feel secure and needed in their job. When one is successful in their job, they are that person that is needed by all, they are the one that gets compliments from everyone, they are the one that can be relied upon to get things done, they are the most important person in that organization as everybody uses them. If a Christian can do this in his worldly job, he can definitely do this in his spiritual job. What if this Christian were so sold out for God that their every being was focused on God and they only worked here or there to get by on, what a state of revival this nation would experience? Here in the United States, Christians have really never had to experience want in their lives. We live in a land that has been blessed with plenty. There are always jobs out there, there is always money to be made. It is getting focused on the culture and sacrificing the things of God that our genie rewards us with when we choose to serve him.

Let's now go to the Word of God to see what Jesus said about this genie's idea of happiness. *Matthew 6:19-21 Lay not up for yourselves treasures upon earth, where moth and rust doth corrupt, and where thieves break through and steal:* Jesus is very clear he says NOT to build up treasures here in this earth. If you look and watch when a person dies, and they have a lot of stuff the family tends to fight over this stuff. I have seen a lot of Gods children do the same, they want the stuff that the parents have worked for their life so they can have what they believe is the financial success in their lives, most of the time this only leads to more misery and destruction as their focus is still on the genie god and not the God of the bible. When I die, all that will be left for my wife, son, and grandchildren is my books which describe my walk with God, my prodigal years, and Gods love and restoration for an old sinner that got his heart and life focused on the God of the bible and how that God of the bible transformed this old man's life. This is laying up treasures in Heaven. This is stuff that will keep going. Sure, these books will sit on bookshelves for many years but sooner or later someone that God wants to read them will find them and they will be just what the person needs at that exact time in their lives to get to God. All the material possessions that my wife and I own is maybe, on the high side worth $500 yard sale value. We are so happy with each other because the God of the bible is the center of our lives, doing his work is the center of our lives, seeing souls come to Jesus is the center of our lives, and the stuff is just stuff. It comes and goes.

This is what Jesus is saying here. Don't focus on things that will fall away, don't focus on things that people can steal, focus on God. If someone breaks into my house to steal things, they will be so disappointed in what they find that they might just leave me a check thinking I am in need. (insert laugh here)

The genie god will have your focus so much on him that all you desire is to lay up treasure on this earth. You goal in life will be on thigs and stuff, that bigger house, that nicer car, that more expensive restaurant. That genie will get you so focused on these thigs that you will not be able to see that you are sacrificing your family time, you are sacrificing the Great Commission what the God of the bible asked you to do, you will no longer have a problem missing church, missing prayer meeting will no longer bother you, you will be just like everyone else trying to get things you cannot afford, with money you don't have to impress people you don't like. This is the result of your genie god.

But lay up for yourselves treasures in heaven, where neither moth nor rust doth corrupt, and where thieves do not break through nor steal: The treasure that a child of God is to lay up for themselves is a treasure of eternal value. When a Christian reaches a lost soul and shares the gospel of Jesus Christ with that soul and that lost person accepts Christ as their personal Savior, the bible says that that person is SEALED with the Holy Spirit until the day of redemption. The day of redemption is the day we as the saved meet Jesus, either in our death or in that Blessed hope, the return of Jesus. This meeting of Jesus is in eternity. That is an eternal reward. No man, no device, no government, can destroy any eternal security. No one can break into a person's soul and steal the Holy Spirit out from him. These are the treasures in Heaven we are to lay up for ourselves.

My wife and I at the time of this writing are packing and getting ready to move to New York to pastor a church that the founding pastor had to resign due to serious health issues. I am a working Pastor. When we first learned that we were going to be moving my focus went immediately to stability for the move. The Lord had provided everything we needed, but I, by my nature was focused on a job first. I am a truck driver by trade. I applied for jobs all over the area where we are to pastor and even had been interviewed by a few companies. You may say that is all good. I would say yes, it is, but then the Lord started to work on my heart and through my wife the Lord had to show me to slow down a little to make sure I am laying up eternal treasure not earthly treasure.

Here in Colorado, we had not had the church started yet, so I had to work first then build the church. Doing it this way I was sacrificing things of the ministry to keep the job. This was part of the boot camp that I refer to this Colorado ministry as. The church in NY is an established church that needs someone to work it. if I am working my job based on what I know it will end up in the same place as this ministry is. Some will get saved but there will be those I won't reach due to working. The Lord allowed me to have at least three months of my regular paycheck coming in due to unemployment and the government increases. Plus, my company covers all my health insurance for this time as well. So, God said slow down I am paying you to get settled, to get thew church settled, and I will show you what the next step is. If I focus on the church first as God has called me to do, the job, whatever it is will be just enough to provide what we need without sacrificing any part of the ministry. The genie god says work and only put half effort into the church, the God of the bible says put all your effort into my church and I will more than abundantly provide what you need. This choice is simply mine to make, but God is not going to move us to do the exact same thing we are doing here I have a full-time job here and a part time ministry here, there we need to have a full-time ministry, and a part time job.

For where your treasure is, there will your heart be also. Where any person even a child of God puts their treasure, there their heart will be also. Treasure simply defined is: something of great worth or value. Look over your life, what is of great worth to you? Is it your wife, your Children, your Job, is it your church or your walk with God, only you know? Then as you answer that question then find the proof. Look at your financial records, what do you spend the most of your money on, do you spend more money on your nice vehicles, do you spend your money on improving things in your house that you could live without, do you spend most of your time at work and working some at home even when you are off. All these are tough to discover. Then you must compare what you spend your money on to what are you giving or doing for God and the ministry of your local church. Are you even giving at least the ten percent model that is illustrated in Malachi, are you giving willingly of the increase of your goods, or are you just giving the bare minimum to the church of your time and money? How about that marriage of yours, are you more in love with your job and the importance you feel at that job or the money you make, do you spend more time dwelling on those things than you do your wife, where is your great worth or value put? Most of Gods children put their treasure into the world and what it has to offer because they have fallen in love with a genie god that makes them feel good and have rebelled against the God of the bile that convicts their hearts and gets their focus on him. Where is your treasure?

SELFISH PRIDE

Proverbs 16:18-19 Pride goeth before destruction, and an haughty spirit before a fall.

The genie god that most of us long for develops one result in each and every person that seeks after him, that one result is simply pride. Many Christians struggle with pride. We are all very good at seeing pride in each other while at the exact same time we refuse to see the pride in ourselves. We are all very quick to pass the judgment of pride on someone else. We will condemn that person, we will gossip about that person, and we will form groups to remove that person from places of leadership. While we at the same we cling to a super spiritual role and show people how special we are in the Lord. Which this is a prideful thing in itself.

There was a man a couple of years ago that came through our ministry here in Colorado. He had been a prodigal just like I was, and he had the display that he had been humbled and was now chasing the God of the bible. I honestly believed that he was genuine. He had been in church before, he had surrendered to God's ministry many years prior. So, after some time I ordained him as an Evangelist. I was still a new Pastor and learning how people operate. Once this man was ordained the selfish pride in himself rose to a level I had never seen before. We started to see things going on in his life that did not line up with the bible. He would brag to everyone how he was seeking God, how much time he was spending in the Word of God. He would want to preach all the time, but would always make excuses as to why when the door knocking time came, he could not do it. he worked a full-time job as well. He could work that job with little to no issues but then would always be in pain and could not walk when it came time to evangelize.

He would call other churches to preach the word, but the work of the ministry was far from him. then when he would preach it was always about him and not about God. When a person is truly seeking God, they do not need to tell anyone they are. People will see it in them. They will see God working in their lives. When one has to tell people about it, they have a prideful attitude. This man, as he was on his prideful journey, he had had some blessings come his way. He focused on the raises he got at work, he focused on the popularity he had, at the same time he started to focus on tv and other things and his walk with God began to drift and fall away. I know this because he lived with us during this time.

After the Lord convicting my heart to talk to him about this, he got angry with me, anger is ALWAYS a sign of a prideful heart. He stopped going to church and eventually fell back into the sin of alcohol. Pride will ALWAYS lead to destruction; it will always allow the fake blessings to come to you so you can believe that it is God who is blessing. Remember Satan is the prince of this world. If Satan appeared to man just as he is no one would serve him for they would see him as he truly is, so he must deceive people to get them to serve him. not only does Satan deceive people into serving him, he convinces them that they are happier serving him than the God of the bible. As Satan does not temp people in his natural form, he must use his made-up genie god to grant rebellious sinners their wishes, then this genie god tells them when things fall apart that it was the God of the bible's fault. If a true Child of God is seeking the God of the bible, they will be in the word, and they will be an overcomer and be able to stand against the genie god and resist his temptations. Let's look at some passages from the bible as to what God has to say about pride. Keep in mind the bible was not written for the lost of this world, but for the saved of the world to know how to live for him. the lost (natural man) cannot understand the things of God for they are foolishness to him unless the Holy Spirit reveals it to him. for a natural man, sin, and pride are a normal action, for the saved these choices must be defeated for God to work in one's life.

Psalm 10:4-7 The wicked, through the pride of his countenance, will not seek after God: God is not in all his thoughts. When God is not in the thoughts of people sin will take that place. We by nature since Adam in the Garden of Eden, have a sin nature. When God is not in our thoughts it makes way for our pride to grow.

The genie god will convince you that it is ok to not seek God. He will convince you that he, not the God of the bible, is better to meet your needs when you want him to instead of having to remove the sin from your life to allow the God of the bible to transform your life. The difference between the two gods is simply this, one will once in a while change your situation, the other will always change your life. I served my genie god for many years and now I have chosen to serve the God of the bible which has transformed my life to a peaceful life.

Notice that the bible says that those who do not seek after God or seek after him in all their thought are considered wicked prideful people? What a statement to make. Are you living a prideful selfish way or living God's way? Sometimes when living the way of the God of the bible you get treated badly, things happen that are not fair, others get what you deserved. That is life. My bible says that the God of the bible shall supply ALL my need according to his riches.

His ways are always grievous; thy judgments are far above out of his sight: as for all his enemies, he puffeth at them. The wicked prideful man's ways are always grievous. There is always trouble for the man that choose his genie god to serve. The judgements of the God of the bible are so far out of the sight of the wicked man that he never thinks he is going to get punished for his actions.

There was a time in my life that I did the same thing. I lived in my prideful state, I was serving my genie god to whom I had pledged my allegiance to, I was not concerned at all about the judgements of the God of the bible. This is why God's children go after their genie god instead of him because there is no conviction of the Holy Spirit with a genie. He comes out and sort of answers your requests, and when those issues sometimes get worse, he convinces you to blame the God of the bible for the disobedient choices you made.

He hath said in his heart, I shall not be moved: for I shall never be in adversity. This "I shall not be moved" is talking about that person that is so full of their prideful selfish way that they refuse to move from that position. Along with pride comes arrogance, the bible calls this a haughty spirit. It is a spirit that one displays to show the pride without coming right out with their pride. We have all at one time or another seen or even been that person with this arrogant attitude. These people some of the time are right. If they say "I'm better than you" sometimes they can prove they are. The genie god allows this attitude to build. He never convicts them that they are heading down a destructive path. He just keeps feeding what they want to hear so they will feel good about themselves and not return to the God of the bible. Unfortunately for them the God of the bible has all power on earth and in heaven where the genie god only has the power of the individual serving him. this person usually is not moved away from his pride until a lot of destruction happens.

His mouth is full of cursing and deceit and fraud: under his tongue is mischief and vanity. The genie god loves this in a child of the almighty God. When one is engulfed in any single sin, all sins are no longer an issue for him. if one is engulfed in pride and arrogance, then cursing and deceit will not be any issues for him either.

I knew a man named Ernest Hoag[1] that when he was living in his sin, he had a lawn service landscape business. He was not good at managing the business. He would always price his work so low that he it would cost him money to do a job. He got himself into so much trouble that he intentionally frauded his bank many times by writing checks with no money in the accounts, hoping to get some money in the bank before the check hit the bank. He knew that the bank sometimes would cash the check if it were small enough and just charge him an overdraft fee. He did this so much that he had over two thousand dollars in overdraft fees in one month. This was an intentional action. He was also cussing, blaming the God of the bible for the choice he made which his genie god encouraged him to make. I am very pleased to say that a few years ago that my dear friend Ernest got his heart and life right with the God of the bible, God changed his life, and he is now a Pastor as God had called him to do.

Proverbs 8:13 The fear of the Lord is to hate evil: pride, and arrogancy, and the evil way, and the froward mouth, do I hate. The God of the bible hates evil. He wants his children to follow him, to serve him,

---

[1] See the Authors work: Redemption: A True Life Prodigal, for the complete story of Ernest Hoag.

and to trust him. when a person reverences someone, such as a parent, a mentor, they have the highest respect for this person. They do not want to make this person disappointed in them, they don't want this person to be upset in any way with their actions. This is a reverence fear. This is the fear that the God of the bible wants for us. He is Holy and he wants us to be Holy. The fear of the Lord is to be a fear of not respecting God not a fear of punishment from God. The fear of punishment from God is for that person that has rejected God and the bible.

Proverbs 16:18-19 Pride goeth before destruction, and an haughty spirit before a fall. This is the promise that your genie god will never ever tell you about. That pride you are clinging to will always led to destruction. Read that again it will ALWAYS lead to destruction. It is a promise.

When one is so focused on their pride and enjoy living so much in this sin, they lose focus on the coming judgement on them for this sin. We have seen people in our lives or even currently that are full of pride. Sometimes we never see this verse fulfilled in them and we think God has not kept his promise because the destruction does not seem to come to them. All I can say is the God of the bible is still on the throne. He is still in charge. In Galatians 6:7 the bible tells us NOT to be deceived, it also says that God is not mocked, then a promise is made that says that a man will reap what he sows' We may never see the judgement of God on a prideful man's life, but it is coming, and God knows just the right time to exercise this judgement.

Better it is to be of an humble spirit with the lowly, than to divide the spoil with the proud. The bible is so full of warnings for God's children that it makes it so easy for one to repent and turn back God. Repentance is never easy in itself when one has been entrapped in a sinful lifestyle, but the idea of repenting and turning to the God of the bible is an easy concept for any prodigal soul to return to God.

God says it is better to humble with the lowly. It is better to remember that it is a fearful thing to fall into the hands of the living God. I have experienced in my lifetime both the judgement of God on my life for my rebellious choices, and I have experienced the humbleness with the lowly. I must be honest here, the humbleness with the lowly is a much happier place to be, then on a mountain with the proudful.

Proverbs 13:10 Only by pride cometh contention: but with the well advised is wisdom. Pride brings contention. This contention is against the God of the bible. Contention simply defined is: rivalry. When one is contentious, they are a rival against something. In this case when one is living in their sinful pride, they become a rival against God.

Romans 8:6-7 tells us that a carnal mind, this is the mind of a Christian that is focused on the world. A

Christian that is serving a genie god. The bible says that this carnal mind is at enmity with God. Enmity simply defined is: active hatred or ill will toward something or someone. When a person is living in their sin, they become contentious which is the first step to enmity. The bible says that this contentious person living in sin is a carnal Christian, which is butting heads with the God of the bible. The genie god could care less about you or how you act, as long as he can lead you to be against the God of the bible, he is happy. Sin will always take you farther than you want to go, it will keep you longer than you want to stay, and most of all it will cost you far more than you want to pay.

1 John 2:15-17 Love not the world, neither the things that are in the world. If any man love the world, the love of the Father is not in him. the bible is clear for those of us that are the children of God. We are not to love the world. Loving the world is to love the things of the world. It is to seek after the things of the world. It is to ignore God almighty to cleave to these things. all things will pass away. There is not one single thing on this earth that a Christian has that is actually his. The earth is the Lords and the fullness there of. God has allowed us to manage his stuff that he allows us to use for such a time as this. Everything that is made by man will be destroyed at some point. It will need to be repaired; it will need to be replace. Live in a house for thirty years sooner or later things in it go bad. They have to be replaced.

God never has to be replaced. The eternal treasure we lay up for ourselves, by witnessing, and telling the lost about the hope that is in Jesus, are eternal rewards which can never be destroyed. They will last forever. If we get to the point in our lives that we destroy our genie god and cling to the God of the bible, we will have so much more than we could ever expect. The God of the bible has already promised to meet all our needs. He has promised to make a way. He has promised that we came from dust and will return to dust. He never said we are born of dust and will return to dust with all our stuff. It doesn't work that way.

When a person passes, they leave all their stuff behind. Their family usually fights over the possessions they had, and it causes anger and hatred in the family which only serves a genie god. The God of the bible does not need one single thing in this world in is eternal glory. We are to love the God of the bible and trust him in all things.

For all that is in the world, the lust of the flesh, and the lust of the eyes, and the pride of life, is not of the Father, but is of the world. If our lustful ways are not of God, they must be of Satan. Satan controls the genie god which answers your wants and desires of what this world has to offer. But it is not what the God of the bible wants at all.

In this world we want money, powers, and status. These three things we falsely believe will bring us happiness. If that is the case than why do so many famous movie stars end up killing themselves. They have all the money the world can offer, they are important in most people's eyes, and they have the power of influence, so why may I ask do they kill themselves. It is because any life without the God of the bible will never lead to that happiness that they are longing for. These people kill themselves because they have a void in their hearts that they felt all the sinful worldly things could fill. They were happy at moments as that is what sin does it makes one happy for the moment, but once that moment passes and it always passes, they are still left wanting. They are left with a hole in their hearts that only the God of the bible can fill.

And the world passeth away, and the lust thereof: but he that doeth the will of God abideth for ever. This is the final verse we will discuss in this chapter. It is simply a confirmation of what we have been saying all along. The world, all it has to offer, the sin you are chasing and having your genie god help you with will all pass away. None of it will ever last. Only what is done for Christ will be what is remembered in eternity. Do you want to continue in your sinful way, or do you want to turn from your wicked way, repent of your sin, so the God of the bible can heal your life, your land, and your eternal rewards? **Hebrews 10:31 it is a fearful thing to fall into the hands of the living God.**

PRIDE MOVEMENT

Leviticus 18:22 Thou shalt not lie with mankind, as with womankind: it is an abomination.

This chapter is sure to have some controversy. Sadly, some of the opposition will be among people who claim to be bible believing Christians. Those who read this book and are not saved will also get offended about what the bible actually says about this topic.

It is necessary in this day and age that we must get a couple of points straight before we proceed in this chapter. The God of the bible hates, despises, and rejects the act of homosexuality. It is an abomination to him. Abomination simply defines is: something regarded with disgust or deep hatred. This is how the God of the bible views this act. The God of the bible loves the person that is committing this act, but he has that abomination to their sin.

We also see in the book of Proverbs that there are other sins besides homosexuality that God considers an abomination, let's look at them for a minute ***Proverbs 6:16-19 These six things doth the Lord hate: yea, seven are an abomination unto him: A proud look, a lying tongue, and hands that shed innocent blood, An heart that deviseth wicked imaginations, feet that be swift in running to mischief, A false witness that speaketh lies, and he that soweth discord among brethren.*** Lying, gossip, pride, murder (abortion), bad thoughts, always getting into trouble, these are all considered to be abominations to the God of the bible.

If we each examine our lives, we will see that we have all at times committed these acts against God. In today's world and in Christs Church one of the biggest issues is gossip. It runs amuck in most modern-day churches, and in many bible believing churches. I have personally seen gossip destroy a church. There are NOT different levels of abomination in the bible. Abomination is abomination plain and simple. God hates sin the same for the lost person of the world as he does for the saved person who has chosen to rebel against the things of God.

The God of the bible loves all people as we see in *John 3:16, II Peter 3:9* he loves the sinner but hates the sin. In the passage in II Peter 3:9 he even says that that he does not want ANYONE to perish but that all should come to repentance. Here we see the God of the bible calling for repentance, calling the sinner to turn from his wicked way so God himself can begin to make one Holy in his sight. This is what the God of the bible is about.

Today we in the churches have drifted from what the bible says about the sinner verses the sin, and we have become self-righteous in our presentation of God to the world that we are turning so many people from the Lord at alarming rates. There is a new movement going on in the Independent Baptist church world which I am a Pastor of an independent Baptist church. This new movement which I am most definitely NOT associated with, Is called the (NIFB) standing for the New Independent Fundamental Baptist. In some areas they have drifted from the bible and one of their core principles is that all homosexuals, lesbians, and anyone associated with them should die and go to Hell, that there is no possibility of repentance for them that God hates them. This is simply not a biblical standpoint.

The genie god that everyone wants to serve is the god who will convince you to go against what the Word of

God says. If you are doing anything and it goes against the bible you are serving your genie god. Those that promote the hate the sinner along with the sin, especially in the sin of homosexuality, have taken the story of Sodom and Gomorrah and only focused on the reason for the destruction as described in Genesis chapter 19. To understand the full meaning of the story one must study Genesis 18 in detail.

Genesis 18 outlines how Abraham went to God pleading for God to save the city, which was committing these horrible sins of homosexuality, and asked if he found fifty righteous people would God spare it, and God said he would, then when Abraham could not find the fifty, he went back to God for the forty, then thirty, all the way down to ten. The question must be asked, if God hated the sinner because of the sin then why was God willing to spare the city for the sake of the righteous, even the ten righteous? So, they could witness to the lost, so those committing these acts could have a time of repentance from their sins. The bible has always been about repentance and redemption[2]

The other extreme view on what the bible says that has divided our churches today is tolerance. We have those who have drifted from the bible to the only love side of God. Is what I mean is as we saw above there are those who drifted from the Word of God to only focus on the judgment of God, and that God will destroy

---

[2] See the Authors work, Redemption: A True life Prodigal.

those who commit certain sins, to those that have drifted from the bible to the God is only love movement. This "God is only love" mindset has caused many churches, even bible believing churches, to allow sin into the churches and has caused them to embrace this sin.

The genie god loves division in the church. He will make you feel all happy, he will convince you that tolerating all sin is what God would do and that since Jesus Christ died for all that it does not matter what we do or who we allow into leadership in our churches it is all love. These people also say it is not for us to judge. But the bible says it is sin, and sin has to be called out, and repented of so the God of the bible can forgive, heal, and restore a person. This is the God of the bible.

We must remember as we saw at the beginning of this chapter, no sin is any worse than the other. If you do a word search on the word Abomination, it appears 142 times in the bible and describes all sins at some point. To classify a homosexual as a sinner that is an abomination to God without condemning yourself for your lying and gossip makes you as much of an abominable sinner as the person you are calling an abominable sinner. This is because the genie god we serve convinces us that we are better than everyone else. This is all because of pride. We must now go to the bible to see what it says about the sin of homosexuality and how sinful acts should never be tolerated, and how it has become accepted by

Christians all over the world and is destroying the church that Christ gave his life for. My personal stand is simply this, if the bible says it is sin, then it is sin. Sin will not be tolerated. The sinner will be loved, the sin will not.

Leviticus 18:22 Thou shalt not lie with mankind, as with womankind: it is abomination. This verse leaves no question as to the meaning of what it was saying. In the bible we sometimes have to read ahead of a verse or after a verse to understand the meaning of a verse. One thing about the word of God, if a saved person reads the bible the Holy Spirit will reveal to that person what the meanings are. The bible tells us this. The lost natural man cannot understand these things (I Corinthians 2:14)

This verse simply, plainly, says that man is not to lay with man, as he does with womankind. In simpler words a man is NOT to have a sexual relation with another man as it is a sin and an abomination. Today we have church denominations splitting because they are allowing homosexual clergy be pastors in churches. You can disguise homosexuality all you want, you can take that sin and wrap it up in a priest robe, or behind a pulpit, or even as a boy scout leader, it is still sin. It is no different than an adulterer who has become a Pastor and preaches hard against sin, he has souls saved, he sees people come to Christ, his sin of adultery is still sin of adultery and will get found out one day. The bible tells us that ALL sin gets found out (Numbers 32:23)

Most Christians will stop right here with this verse. They will use this to judge someone for what they do. They will call this homosexual an abomination against God and they need to be destroyed, but they overlook the above verses in Proverbs six. SIN IS SIN, I cannot emphasize that enough and homosexuality is sin. In any form, in any function, in any area. When homosexuality is flaunted in the streets in parades called "Pride" or put on the calendars as "Pride month" it is still sin. My bible tells me that **Proverbs 16:18 Pride goeth before destruction, and an haughty spirit before a fall.** It is God's job to reveal and expose sin. Sin will be revealed, it will be known, and it will be judged. When we as Christian's judge sin we must do it with the same biblical judgement that we would judge ourselves with compare ALL sin to the word of God.

Leviticus 20:13 If a man also lie with mankind, as he lieth with a woman, both of them have committed an abomination: they shall surely be put to death; their blood shall be upon them. In the Old Testament if persons were caught in this sin they were put to death. The reason for this is because the God of the bible hates sin. Whereas your genie god doesn't care that you sin. There were many sins in the Old Testament and even in the New Testament that a person was killed for when they committed these acts.

This verse goes one step farther and says that their blood will be upon them. In other words, those who did the killing of those caught in this sin, would not be held accountable to God for their death. The ones who committed the sins would be the ones held accountable to God. Many today have taken this principle to say that all homosexuals are sinners and need to be killed. There is a Pastor in a church that prays for God to kill these people and that they can never be saved. This is not a biblical position.

One must also remember these passages in the bible are based on the Old Testament law. The sin is just that, it is sin, but the grace of God through the shed blood of Jesus Christ allows forgiveness of sins, for one to be restored to Gods kingdom if they so choose to accept God's grace.

Romans 1:21-32 Because that, when they knew God, they glorified him not as God, neither were thankful; but became vain in their imaginations, and their foolish heart was darkened. We will now go to the New Testament to see some verification of the passages in the Old Testament. This is necessary because there are those who say that the New Testament is what we live by, and that God is only about love, and that love is love. We will see that the genie god is all about love and that all love is love, including homosexual love. The God of the bible loves everyone, but he hates sin at the same time. Sin has to be judged. If sin were not judged, there would be no Hell, there would have been no need for Jesus Christ to have died on that Old rugged cross. There would be no need for salvation. The genie god loves a works-based salvation. A salvation that says if I do good, I can get into Heaven, if I live my life peacefully, I will be ok at the end. This is not what the God of the bible says. The God of the bible says that There is only ONE way to heaven and that is through Jesus Christ. John 14:6

We see here in this verse that the door to sin becomes open when one chooses NOT to glorify the God of the bible. This Pride movement is the farthest thing from the God of the bible, but they are the closest they can be to their genie god. The bible tells us that when they KNEW GOD. This is the God of the bible. Everyone of God creatures, including mankind, have a built-in knowledge that there is a God. It is through sinful choices that a person chooses to reject the things of God. This verse shows that when one goes down that road to sin, they first had a knowledge of God, but they rejected, the God of the bible, they chose not to glorify the God of the bible, and they were no longer thankful for what God has given them. The genie god makes sin so attractive, and enticing, that one will gladly follow and worship him. This attraction seems great and one believes that there are no consequences for choosing to follow this genie god.

A person believes with all their heart that they can follow this genie and serve the God of the bible at the same time. The bible, history, and God has proven that time and time again sin will always lead to destruction. When one stops glorifying (worshiping, honoring, loving, seeking) the God of the bible. They have just opened the door to sin and made room for their genie god. The bible says that their hearts are foolish, and they start to become vain. Vain simply defined is: having or showing excessive pride. Did you read that? Vain leads to pride.

So, let's take a minute and recap. This verse says that when they knew God, they chose to reject God, they stopped being thankful, they became prideful in their imaginations, and their hearts were darkened. The Pride movement has come as a result of being vain in their imaginations, as a result of rejecting the God of the bible. It all starts with a choice. To either cling to the God of the bible or cling to your genie god, I assure you, the God of the bible wins.

Professing themselves to be wise, they became fools, Sin will always have pride attached to it. this pride has destroyed many relationships, many friendships, and has led many good people down a path away from the God of the bible. The first indication of pride is that the person no longer believes the Word of God to be true. They no longer take it for what it says. I spoke to a friend the other day that I have not heard from in many years. One of the first things he let me know was that he was not KJV only anymore and that he believed the new manuscripts were the closest to the originals. Now one foundational disconnect to the "original manuscripts" argument is that the original manuscripts are no longer around so no one can compare anything to them. The bible tells us that God preserves his word in perfect, complete form, unto all generations, so I believe it for what it says until the time it is proven false. I use this example to show that once a little pride wells up inside someone, the very first thing that happens is that they no longer believe the bible for what it says. When one starts to question the Word of God or the bible, this opens the door for sin to get in.

Those supporting the "Pride Movement" have professed themselves wise and all they do is act like fools. The bible says in *Psalms 14:1 The fool hath said in his heart, There is no God. They are corrupt, they have done abominable works, there is none that doeth good.* There is that word abominable again. If anything is done without God, it will be done with pride. The genie god of the pride movement has allowed these people to use scripture they don't believe, to support sin they know is an abomination, to feed their personal pride so they can feel all good about themselves. The God of the bible holds us all accountable.

And changed the glory of the uncorruptible God into an image made like to corruptible man, and to birds, and fourfooted beasts, and creeping things. Throughout the years, history has proven over and over again that when one gets away from the bible and no longer makes it the foundation of their life, than pride gets in. the genie god wants you to serve him, he will make it seem like you are in control of your life, he will make your sin seem very tolerable, and he will tell you that you really are not sinning that badly. This all changes the glory of the God of the bible to the corruptible image made by man. Remember the first Commandment Thou shalt have NO OTHER gods before me? This includes your genie god. The pride movement has changed this glory of God through the natural one-man one-woman marriage design to an evil, nasty, abominable sexual experience that for some seem like it is ok. I cannot say this enough, sin ALWAYS ends in destruction. Homosexuality and the pride movement will end in destruction. The bible says that we are all accountable to God for our own actions. ***Romans 14:12 So then every one of us shall give account of <u>himself</u> to God.*** This is the God of the bible. The genie god will be nowhere to be found at this judgement. Did you notice that it said that a man must give an account of HIMSELF to GOD?

Those choosing to live this sinful lifestyle, know they are living in sin, they are mocking God by living in their sin, they are going against the very nature of their bodies, and thy know it. God designed certain things that are natural actions. For example, if one is on the edge of a cliff and they began to lose footing, they immediately, by nature, will do whatever they can with whatever they have, to save their lives. This is by nature. A man has a natural desire for a woman, and a woman has a natural desire for a man. When this changes it is because pride has gotten in the way, and the genie god has convinced them they know better than the God of the bible and the God of the bible does not want them to be happy, because love is love as they say.

Wherefore God also gave them up to uncleanness through the lusts of their own hearts, to dishonour their own bodies between themselves: when a person serves their genie god for so long the God of the bible will let them alone for some time. He still sees what is happening, he still knows what is going on, but he lets these folks wander for however long it takes for them to destroy their lives, and then turn back to him. there are and will continue to be some that will never make the change back to God here on this earth, but the moment they step into eternity, they will realize that this genie lied to them every step of the way.

In this verse we see that God gives a person up to their own sin, because of the evil lusts of their hearts, and allows them to dishonor their own bodies. Our bodies are designed to be the temple of God. The bible tells us in I Corinthians 3:16-18 that we (our bodies) are a temple of God and that if we defile that temple that God shall destroy that temple for it was designed to be Holy to him.

Who changed the truth of God into a lie, and worshipped and served the creature more than the Creator, who is blessed for ever. Amen. Sin again changes the truth that the God of the bible established and turns it into a lie. The genie will always lie, he only looks out for himself, he is an agent of Satan who only wants to destroy you. Ever notice how Satan never goes after the wicked or the lost, he only goes after those who are the children of God. See, Satan does not need to go after the lost, he did that once in the garden of Eden and those choices made all mankind doomed for all eternity, unless they accept Jesus as their Lord and savior.

For this cause God gave them up unto vile affections: for even their women did change the natural use into that which is against nature: And likewise also the men, leaving the natural use of the woman, burned in their lust one toward another; men with men working that which is unseemly, and receiving in themselves that recompence of their error which was meet. When a person continues in their sin, after a while God gives them to their sin. Sin begins to harden one's heart. and a person that knows what God expects and chooses to do the opposite after a while will have to live in that sin for quite a while. While some don't return back to God on this earth, there are some who do. Those who do not turn back to God on this earth I cannot say that they are not saved as only God himself knows a person's heart. All I do know for sure is the bible teaches that it is appointed unto man ONCE to die and then after his death there will be a judgement (Hebrews 9:27) and that everyman must give an account of himself to God.

We see at the beginning of this passage in Romans 1:21 that the people being talked about are those that know God. This can only mean those who have a relationship with God. This would be those who have entered into this carnal state of mind and are enjoying their sin. The bible is clear that the natural man cannot understand the things of God they are foolishness to him. the lost man will usually reject the things of God, the very idea of God, whereas the child of God knows better but chooses to ignore that anyway. Here is a verse that says something about knowing what to do. *James 4:17 Therefore to him that knoweth to do good, and doeth it not, to him it is sin.* The man that knows to do good is the saved man, because he knows God and when he chooses not to do it, he sins. It is my conviction that this verse also talks about a double accountability for the saved person. First a person will be held accountable for their sin because their sin comes by nature, it was tainted from Adam in the garden of Eden. Then once a person gets saved, he has the knowledge of God for it is spiritually discerned (I Corinthians 2:14)

In this passage God gives these intentional rebellious sinners up to their vile affections. Vile simply defined is: Morally despicable. God allows one to wonder in this sin. As one wonders and lives in their sin, they also reap on themselves the consequences of this sin. The bible says it is a FEARFUL thing to fall into the hands of the living God.

The genie god of this world says yes, the pride movement is a way of life, they say, "we are born this way" they say, "love is love" and the majority of the world buys this mind set. It is a sad day in the United States when we have supposedly godly denominations of churches splitting because some allow the homosexuals in the pastorate and others do not. The bible says it is sin, that settles it, it is sin. We have stopped believing the bible for what it says, we have started to question everything the bible says, and we have blamed it on the "translators" of the word of God. If we believe the bible translators were inspired by the Holy Spirit to interpret the word of God as God told them to then we must believe that God did what he said he would do and preserved his word for ALL generations. The genie god will tell you that no one single translation of the word of God is completely accurate. My bible tells me that Gods word is complete, perfect, and inspired by him to all generations. I believe it for what it says. If the bible says that the God of the bible will turn a rebellious sinner over to his uncleanness than know that God will do that. Your genie god will convince you otherwise. The secret to fighting the genie god is to stay in the book of the God of the bible, to study it, to read it, to learn it, to live it, to love it.

And even as they did not like to retain God in their knowledge, God gave them over to a reprobate mind, to do those things which are not convenient; Reprobate simply defined is: depraved. This verse says that they did not LIKE to retain God in their knowledge. Meaning that the closer they got to their sin, the less of God they wanted in their lives. The Word of God will either draw people closer to the God of the bible, or it will cause them to run as fast as they can away from him. The genie god welcomes all to serve him, the genie has no consequences to offer for their service, the genie tells everyone they will feel good about themselves, the God of the bible convicts, and turns old sinners into glorified saints.

Again, the God of the bible turns people over to their sin, to do the most ungodly, awful, unnatural thigs that could ever be considered. Remember in the days of Noah, the bible says that every thought of the IMAGINATION was only evil continually? (Geneses 6:5)

Being filled with all unrighteousness, fornication, wickedness, covetousness, maliciousness; full of envy, murder, debate, deceit, malignity; whisperers, Backbiters, haters of God, despiteful, proud, boasters, inventors of evil things, disobedient to parents, Without understanding, covenantbreakers, without natural affection, implacable, unmerciful: Who knowing the judgment of God, that they which commit such things are worthy of death, not only do the same, but have pleasure in them that do them. When we ignore the commandments of the God of the bible, the genie god will convince you that you will have pleasure in the evilness of this world.

A person on earth living in his sin, taking pleasure in his genie, and clinging to and living for the evilness of this sinful world, can live his whole life on earth like that. We often ask ourselves; how can this be. Why does God let them live that way? That answer is simple, the God of the bible holds YOU and YOU alone accountable for YOUR actions. He does not hold you accountable for the actions or choices of others. He did not call you to be responsible for the choice's others make. The God of the bible is an all seeing, an all-knowing God and not one single thing gets past home. Just like you after these evil people die, they too will fall into the hands of the living God, the God of the bible, and he and he alone has every right and authority to judge those who we would like to see judged on this earth.

You can be absolutely assured that before the God of the bible exercises his judgement that he has given that person every opportunity to turn from his sin, he has given them many times over and over again the times to repent, he has given his child that rebels against him many opportunities to turn from his sin, but if they don't turn from their sin on this earth they will be judged after this life is over and they are into eternity. This is the God of bible. He is not willing that ANYONE should perish, he wants Everyone, even the most evil acting person, to come to him. (II Peter 3:9)

One last thought, the bible is very clear that Homosexuality, Lesbianism, genderism, and whatever name you try to justify it by, is sin. It is an abomination that is against the God of the bible. It is against his nature. If you are reading this and living in this lifestyle, there is still time. You can kill your genie god and start to cling to the God of the bible. The God of the bible loves you very much, he wants you to love him, and you are NOT born a way that goes against him, that my friend is a choice. If you don't believe me, then I challenge you take three months and seek God with all your heart and ask God to help you fall in love with him, and you will be surprised how your sinful desires will change back to the desires that the God of the bible built in you.

GENDER IDENTITY

Mark 10:6 But from the beginning of the creation God made them male and female.

This chapter is sure to have some controversy as well as the last one did. For whatever strange reason this has become a focus point in our nation. It is a very sad day in any nation that has to have legislation, or presidential executive orders for boys and girls to be forced to use the same bathroom. This day we have men claiming to be women. They dress like women, they act like women, they expect everyone to treat and call them women and they have legal protection that if you don't you can get into trouble.

We have children being forced to have sex changes if they may play with stuff of the opposite sex. It has even been said that children as young as eight years old are competent enough to decide if they want to be a boy or a girl. When a child legally can't vote until they are eighteen, they cannot get a driver's license until age sixteen. These age limits are put in place for the maturity of the child. I don't care who you are, I don't care if you are offended by my statement, no child eight years of age has the mental capability to determine if they want to be a boy or a girl.

We have federal funded prisons, allowing full grown men, who "claim" to be women to have sex changes and to be placed in women's prisons because they "were made a woman" this is the biggest bunch of babbling bull junk I have ever heard in my life. For one to say that they were born a boy but are really a girl, and to have a sex change is to slap the God of the bible in the face and to proclaim that God made a mistake when he created these people that way.

I will say the God of the bible is perfect, and that those who mock and slap the God of the bible in the face are living in sin and are deliberately intentionally rebelling against the things of God. The bible says in ***Galatians 6:7 Be not deceived; God is NOT MOCKED: for whatsoever a man soweth, that shall he also reap.*** Did you see that? First of all don't be deceived. God may allow this evil to continue for a while. It looks at times as God is not doing anything about the evil that is taking place in this world. We must remember two things about this, the first is that God wants everyone to repent and get saved, the second thing for the delay of his judgement is to give folks time to repent of their sin and turn to him. let's look at ***II Peter 3:9 The Lord is not slack concerning his promise, as some men count slackness; but is longsuffering to us-ward, not willing that any should perish, but that all should come to repentance.***

II Peter 3:9 The Lord is not slack concerning his promise, The Lord here is the God of the bible not some genie god that makes you drift from the bible, this is the living God to whom it is fearful to fall into the hands of the living God. The bible says that he is NOT SLACK concerning his promise. What does that mean "not slack?" it simply means that God has to judge sin, there are those that will have to go to the Lake of Fire for their sins. There are those who will reject the gospel, and there are those that are saved but rebel against the things of God, and those who are living for God. He will judge them all. The bible tells us that we will all stand before God, each and every one of us, and that when we do stand before God, we will have to answer not for our neighbor, not for our friends but for ourselves. This is the promise that God made, and he will follow through with it.

as some men count slackness; but is longsuffering to us-ward, there are those that suggest that God won't do anything because he has not done anything so far. We pray for God to judge this world, but we neglect that he must judge us as well for our sins. We blame God for not bringing swift visible judgement upon the sinners of this world while we hide and bury our sin at the same time. This is because men have believed their genie god and have clung to him because he will not judge them for their choices. When a man dresses like a woman, or a woman like a man and they begin to live like that the bible says it is an ABOMINATION against

God. The thing that causes a deliberate rejection and mockery of God is pride. The bible says that pride goeth before destruction we are witnessing the destruction of a once godly nation before our very eyes.

This verse says that the God of the bible is LONGSUFFERING to us. Longsuffering simply defined is: patient. God is patient with us. With people. He loves all people, not just some. As there will only be some that accept his free gift of salvation, most will reject him. he still loves them. No different than a parent that has two children. One turns out pretty good the other always in jail, on drugs, living in sin, you love both of them, but both of them have not always done what they needed to do. This is the being longsuffering.

 not willing that any should perish, but that all should come to repentance. It is clear that God is delaying his punishment to allow as many souls to come to him as possible. His judgment is coming, but he is a loving God. The delay in his judgment shows his absolute love to us as mankind. If God were not a loving God, he would have to kill each person the very moment they committed the smallest of a sin. There would be no one alive. For God to be true if he were just a judging God and not a loving God he cannot tolerate or allow one drop of sin to be in a person's life, if he created them and just one of them committed the smallest of any sin they would have to be destroyed. Sin makes God unhappy. There would be no one left on the earth. As a loving God he is also a just God. He wants all to repent and turn to him, but he will judge them also. Ask yourself this question, why do people who reject God end up in the Lake of fire for all eternity? Because God has to judge sin. If he were not a loving God that judgement would have to be implemented immediately upon the smallest of violations at the moment the violation took place.

As we expound on this for a moment a genie god will ONLY promote a loving God and not a judging God. By having only, a loving God one can do whatever they want with no consequences and believe that they can live their life full of their sin and God will just allow them to enter in his perfect sinless abode. This is where mankind has made its biggest mistake of all time. By believing they can have actions without accountability. This is why we have the homosexuals and transgenders flaunting and promoting their sin because their genie god has convinced them that this is the way the God of the bible wanted it. The bible says this is sin, so it is sin.

Deuteronomy 22:5 The woman shall not wear that which pertaineth unto a man, neither shall a man put on a woman's garment: for all that do so are abomination unto the Lord thy God.

Deuteronomy 22:5 The woman shall not wear that which pertaineth unto a man, this verse in the bible is pretty clear. It says that Woman shall not wear that, which means anything, that pertaineth to a man.

Pertain simply defined is: an accessory or product. This day and age where we have people getting sex change operations, we have allowed for identity applications that requires sex identification to include "other" including male and female, this is the most anti-God, anti-Bible, and anti-Nature thing that we have ever done in society. The bible says it is sin, then for those of you reading this who may get offended I must say it is sin as the bible says it is.

Sin cannot honor God as God is a Holy God. Holy meaning perfect and sinless. This is the God of the bible. As his children we are washed in the blood of Jesus Christ, and we are to present our bodies, Holy and acceptable to Him. (Romans 12:1-2) when we choose to disobey God's standards and his commands we sin and there will be consequences. When the God of the bible says it is sin, the genie god will say it is ok, and that the God of the bible made a mistake when he created a person that has made the choice to live the same sex lifestyle.

It is my understanding that in every same-sex relationship that there is one dominate partner which represents a man and one less dominate partner which represents a woman in the relationship. Looking at it like this let's explore a thought for a moment. Why are both the men in a homosexual relationship not the dominate and why are both woman in a lesbian relationship not dominate or in this case the weaker vessel? It is because they are comparing themselves to a standard heterosexual relationship. In a normal relationship God designed the man to be the stronger vessel and he designed the woman to be the weaker vessel. Since, in every gay relationship, they feel they must compare themselves to the standard of the heterosexual relationship. I have this same issue with different versions of the bible. I am a King James Bible only person. That is me, it is my choice, and I am standing strong on this point. The other versions of the bible leave out verses in the bible. Instead of renumbering their bible they hide the missing verses in the text. If they TRULY believed that their NEW bible was more accurate, and they stood behind it, then why not renumber it? the reason is because they knew that people would reject it, as all other bibles are compared to the KJV which is and has always been the standard for the Word of God. All the other versions would be rejected by man if they renumbered their bibles. This would the same in these ungodly, sinful, same sex unions, if both males were dominate, they would fight and almost kill each other and the women would hate each other, God designed a man and a woman to complement and complete each other. In a same sex union, it is impossible for this union to be complete there will always be a void.

neither shall a man put on a woman's garment: for all that do so are abomination unto the Lord thy God. The God of the bible is clear here, it says to do this is an abomination to Him. there is no way to misunderstand this verse. There is no way to be confused about this verse. There is no way one can question this verse as who it applies to and who it is revealment for today, it says what it says, and the God of the bible says it is sin. Men are not to wear women's clothes neither are women to wear men's clothes.

In the United States we have put in place one of the most ungodly presidents in all of American history. He and the news organizations are making a big deal about this HE/SHE that has been appointed as the leading health expert in our nation. This God rejector gets on tv and flaunts his sin in front of the whole world by wearing long hair designed to look like a woman, woman's clothes, including the makeup, he calls himself a woman's name and the lost world accepts this and a lot of "Christians" are saying that love is love and this is ok and that God will be his judge. To that point they are correct the bible does say that every person will answer for themselves at the judgement.

When one sees this sin being flaunted and promoted, you can see the sin all over it. This is what the genie god wants, he wants you to be comfortable in your sin. He wants you to reject the God of the bible because the genie god is controlled by Satan. If you are away from a solid relationship with the God of the bible you will fall in love with this genie god and say that you hate Satan, while at the same time clinging to him and not even knowing it.

Since this verse has been crystal clear and one still chooses to go this kind of a lifestyle it is a deliberate, intentional rejection and rebellion against the God of the bible. The bible tells us NOT to be deceived that God, the God of the bible, is NOT mocked, meaning that soon enough one's sin will catch up to them and there will be a judgement, and this judgement will not be good. At the judgement when the very first Sodomite or Lesbian are sentenced to eternity in the Lake of Fire separated from the God of the bible for all eternity for rejecting him, then all the other will all of a sudden no longer be in that lifestyle, they will cry, scream, make any and all excuses they think that God will accept to only find their eternal fate the same. This will truly be a sad day.

God is loving enough that he allows for one to repent of his sin and turn to God, he can forgive them, and change them, there are many testimonies of people who have done this. There are a very small few of these folks who have at one time accepted Christ as their Saviour, who are living in life of rebellion. I truly believe there will be a double accountability for the saved person who rebels as the bible says that for those of us who know to do good and do not do it, then it is sin (James 4:17) As this chapter is about gender, we must have the same conversation as we have had about the previous chapter as the two go hand in hand.

Matthew 19:4 And he answered and said unto them, Have ye not read, that he which made them at the

beginning made them male and female, here is what Jesus had to say about genderism. He was asking the pharisees who were trying to get him to say something opposite of that scriptures about divorce and remarriage[3] if they had read that when God had made the very first people in the world that he made them male and female only. He did make Adam and Eve in the Garden of Eden not Adam and Steve. Jesus says that God made them in the beginning, this beginning is the beginning of time itself, he mad one man and one woman to live together in this life. He did not design, nor did he allow nature to be designed to allow two men as a couple and two women as a couple. It is sin, the bible says it is sin, so therefore when one engages in changing their gender they are living in a sinful, godless, God-rejecting, God-rebelling life, that they will stand before the God of the bible and have to answer for. The bible says it is a FEARFUL thing to fall into the hands of the living God. This living God is NOT a genie which is controlled by Satan, it is the God of the bible.

Mark 10:6 But from the beginning of the creation God made them male and female. Just in case there are still those who are arguing that God made a mistake on how he created them, that the word beginning means the beginning of maturity, or whatever poppycock one can dream of, the bible in this verse goes on to add that when God made man and woman, he made them from the beginning of CREATION. This

---

[3] See the authors work The Biblical Family: From Beginning to Blended

was and is the design. Mankind can try with all his limited might to change what the God of the bible has established, they can try to force others to accept it as well, but all their best efforts and might will never hold a dimmer of a glow of a candle at the judgement[4] that we will all have to stand before God at.

ABORTION

Jeremiah 1:5 Before I formed thee in the belly I knew thee; and before thou camest forth out of the womb I sanctified thee, and I ordained thee a prophet unto the nations.

This is a subject that should never be up for debate in the Christian world, yet it is. There are those that say they are Christian who support this heinous act of murdering an unborn baby. When the truth is told the

---

[4] When I use the word judgement, I am referring to both biblical judgements. The Great White Throne judgement for the unsaved, and the judgement seat of Christ for those of us who are saved.

reason that people murder their unborn babies is to cover their sin of fornication. Fornication is having sex with a person to whom you are not married to. If there were no fornication, there would be no abortion.

As we get going, I want to make one thing clear, when I use the word abortion, I am referring to the murder of an unborn baby, for the sake of wording of this kind of long book I will use the word abortion.

In the age of the flood in Noah's time in the bible the world was destroyed because every thought and intent of their hearts were evil continually. (Genesis 6:5) This meant that every thought, action, conversation was always talking and doing evil. As abortion is a symptom of a greater sin, it is in itself a sin as well. The bible tells us on many occasions that we as people were formed IN the womb, which means we were alive. When the "knowledgeable" people refer to the living child as a Fetus, or a mass of cells they are telling others that the God of the bible is a liar and that the baby is not alive in the womb until that child is born.

In our nation at this very moment, abortion is being praised, it is being forced upon society to accept, it is being used to mock God at the highest level. People (God's creation) believe they are more knowledgeable than God, they have better answers than God, and they refuse to accept him as their God. The bible tells us in Numbers 32:23 to be sure that our sins will find us out. There is coming a day, when all will be exposed for what it is, there is coming a day when all will be judged for what it is, there is coming a day when all judgements will be fulfilled. Make no mistake about it the bible has been and always will be true, God will be found to be true, and every man will be found to be a liar. (Romans 3:4)

I was strolling through my news feed this morning and came across a sing from a group that is supporting abortion, and, on their sign, it said "if Mary had had an abortion, we would not be in this mess" just think about this, these people are trying to justify their sin of fornication that they are blaming their sin on our Lord and Saviour Jesus Christ. I praise God for their sakes that he is a loving merciful, and a just God and that because of his love he is giving these folks a little more time to repent. If they still choose to reject him, they will be judged. God has to judge sin, or he would not be God, he has to allow for repentance, or he would not be love, this is who God is. When we begin to blame God for our choices it is because we refuse to accept the responsibility for those choices. Be assured God has tuff shoulders, remember what the bible says *John 1:11 He came unto his own, and his own received him not.* This is where we are at today in our society is that Jesus is come unto those he loves, to those that love him, to those that hate him, but he still loves them. When he is rejected by the masses, he still keeps loving them, knowing that he will have to punish them for their sins if they do not turn from their wicked ways.

As we could spend many pages on this subject on the evils of murdering unborn babies, we will focus on what the bible says about abortion and we will let the bible be our guide on this. A person that rejects the sanctity of a human life is worshiping a genie god. To prove this, a genie god convinces you that you want to be happy, that you do not want to accept the responsibility of your choices, that you only want what makes you feel good, and that is what abortion does, it eliminates all responsibility, accountability, and is a sin in the eyes of almighty God. Remember this, having an abortion does not mean that you are not a parent, it simply means that you are a parent of a dead baby. I just praise God that these innocent murdered unborn babies are finding themselves in eternity with Jesus without having to experience the evilness of this sinful world. (Isaiah 7:15-16)

Jeremiah 1:5 Before I formed thee in the belly I knew thee; and before thou camest forth out of the womb I sanctified thee, and I ordained thee a prophet unto the nations. This verse is talking about the human soul. The soul is who we are. It is our emotions, our thoughts, it is what controls our brain, it is what operates our bodies. If the soul leaves the body the body begins to rot, it is lifeless, the souls is the life of the body.

God tells Jeremiah here that BRFORE he was formed in the belly. God says before your lifeless body, before your flesh and bones, before you take a deep breath of air, I formed you. He is saying that the soul, which is the life of the body, was formed before the body was. This proves beyond a doubt that life is actually begun before conception. Life is from God, I don't care if it is formed as a result of sinful actions of fornication, evil actions of rape, or blessed actions of marriage, life, all life, is formed by God. The God of the bible.

For man to disregard what God made is a result of sinful selfish pride that a genie god instills in a person to get them away from the word of God. The bible tells us that faith comes by hearing and that hearing comes by the WORD OF GOD. If people are not reading and studying their bibles, they are not increasing their faith. If they are not increasing their faith, they are living in sin before the God of the bible who has to judge them one day because of their sin.

If a person disregards a human life and has an abortion, is this person sentenced to Hell for all eternity? No. they have the opportunity to repent, and God has promised that all those that repent of their sins will be forgiven. **The problem is that no one wants to repent**. The genie god does not want people to repent, he will offer them a feel-good repentance as he does in the Catholic world of taking your sinful actions and confessing them to a sinful man so this sinful man can cleanse you and make you perfect in the sight of God. Please let me know how that works, the only one that can make a sinner whole in the eyes of God is a perfect sinless God. Not a sinful man.

God goes on to say in the bible that after he formed Jeremiah, while Jeremiah was still in the womb, inside his mothers' belly, as a separate being, not "my body" as the women who rebel and reject God say. Their excuse is "my body, my choice" no it is a separate body. Let's use basic science. If it is a woman's body, then if a baby was killed it should kill her as there is a heartbeat, movement, blood pumping. It should require surgery and recovery time, it should require a long healing process if a person, was just a part of your body to remove that part would be very intense. If a person has a tumor, a growth, as a baby is termed, it requires, biopsies, surgery, and recovery time. To kill an unborn baby requires fifteen minutes in a clinic, where a baby is sucked through as vacuum tube as he is ripped apart going through that tube.

If it were not a baby then why when the doctor searches for all the parts of the "fetus" baby, he looks for hands, arms, feet, and a head? It is a separate individual person. Second thing to look at through science is if the baby were part of the woman's body, then why does it have a separate DNA. A completely separate, individual DNA. If it were part of the woman's body, it would have her DNA in it. it is because even as science has proven what the God of the bible says that baby in that mother's belly is a separate, living, creation of God. When this is ignored, rejected, and rebelled against it is because of sin. The genie god loves when a person refuses to accept the responsibility for their choices.

Many Christians have gotten callus to this point and have just accepted it. If parents would hold their children accountable and teach them and monitor them and get them to stop committing the sinful acts of fornication, then abortions would go away. I am in no way saying that if a person is committing the sinful act of fornication, that it is the fault of the parents, I am saying that parents refuse to invest the time, as difficult as it can be, into their children to teach them what the God of the bible has to say about fornication.

Psalm 22:10 I was cast upon thee from the womb: thou art my God from my mother's belly. The bible is clear that it is God that creates life, it is God that makes us who we are. It is God that formed us even before we were born. This verse does not say that God changed the mother, or that God placed the soul of this baby through the mother. It says that HE, the God of the bible, gave life to the baby while the baby was in his mother's womb.

I have had some conversations lately with people, some about losing your salvation, some about this or that but at the end if the bible says it is so, and you chose not to believe, that is just rebellion of the Word of God. We are all built with an inward knowledge of God from our birth. We have it instilled in our very being that there is a creator. The bible tells us in Psalm 150:6 it says let EVERYTHING that has breath Praise the Lord. Everything includes the unborn baby, the born baby, the child, the adult, the animals, the plants, the trees, everything. If all these things that breathe are to praise the Lord, they have some knowledge that there is a Lord. It is through rebellious education that people have rejected the Word of God and have changed it to meet their needs.

Murdering unborn babies is one of those things that is the changing of God's Word; to conform to a sinful rebellion of the Word of God which worships the genie god that one loves to serve. When one murders and unborn baby, they are murdering a baby that God has created, that God has formed, that God himself gave life to. Yes, we as a society worship the slaughter of the innocent, the mockery of the God of the bible and we flaunt our sinful pride and shake our fists in the very face of the almighty God of the bible. My bible says in Galatians 6:7 to not be deceived, because the God of the bible is not mocked, and that sooner or later the God of the bible will execute judgement on this evil wicked nation of ours.

Job 31:15 Did not he that made me in the womb make him? and did not one fashion us in the womb? Here is more proof that life comes for the God of the bible. We are fashioned in the mother's womb. By fashioned it is meant that we get our personalities, our habits, our desires, from inside the womb. Some people grow up to become police officers, some to be truck drivers, some to be Pastors, some to be politicians, all because we were fashioned in the mother's womb.

Psalm 139:13-15 For thou hast possessed my reins: thou hast covered me in my mother's womb. I will praise thee; for I am fearfully and wonderfully made: marvellous are thy works; and that my soul knoweth right well. My substance was not hid from thee, when I was made in secret, and curiously wrought in the lowest parts of the earth. This is a little more of the same that God created life in the womb. It is said in society that a "Fetus" has no life until it breaths air. The bible says it has life before breathing air. Have you ever heard of a baby leaping in the mother's stomach? Have you ever heard of an ultrasound and listening to the baby's heartbeat, how can a baby leap in the womb, or how can it have a heartbeat if it has no life prior to being born? That answer is simple, it is impossible. It is only through sinful rebellion that one rejects what the bible says and focuses on what the god of self, the genie god tells them to believe. The genie god will ALWAYS convince you that your sin is ok.

Hosea 12:3 He took his brother by the heel in the womb, and by his strength he had power with God: Now we must look at life inside the womb for a moment. If a baby does not have a life until it breathes oxygen, then this verse in the bible would be a lie, along with another we will discuss in a minute. This verse proves that a baby has a thought process in the womb, he has a natural built-in desire to survive, and that he is ALIVE in the womb regardless of what sinful rebellion says otherwise.

This verse is referring to Jacob and Esau in the bible. These boys were twins and when Esau was born, and on his way out of his mothers' belly, we see that Jacob grabbed the heal of Esau, he took his brothers heal. He knew enough to hold on. Jacob in the bible was known as a deceiver, that repented, and God used to establish his blood line through.

This verse clearly shows that there is life inside the womb. And to destroy that life is an abomination against God himself. The genie god, the god that is controlled by Satan will convince a person that there is no life, that you can live in sinful sexual acts, and lifestyles and just eliminate the consequences. The God of the bible says it is sin. You believe what you want, all I am saying is that the God of the bible is still on his throne, he is still in charge, he is still King of kings and Lord of lords, and he will judge the sin of this world and the people that commit these sins. God is delaying that judgement to allow these people who are rebellious to him to repent and turn to him as God is not willing that ANY should perish, but that all should come to him. this is the truest form of love from the God of the bible.

Luke 1:31 And, behold, thou shalt conceive in thy womb, and bring forth a son, and shalt call his name JESUS. We see here that the womb is a very special place as this is where God himself forms each and every person. The womb is the place in which he sent his son Jesus to enter this world to be the sacrifice for our sins. The womb is the most sacred part on a woman's body, and it has been used as a battleground to promote sin is against the very nature of God. We see in the bible that baby murder has been since bible times, we saw that even Moses in the bible was hid in the bullrushes so he would not be killed. In the books of the Kings and Chronicles in the bible we read of baby sacrifice, and today in this great nation of the United States of America the Land of the free and the home of the brave, we have declared a war on unborn babies and now that has led to murdering them legally up to an hour after they are born. We are blaming and killing the result of our sinful choice while clinging to those sinful choices. The bible tells us that sin is fun, but it is only for a season, once that season come to an end there is ALWAYS a lifetime of destruction that follows that sin. For some that destruction come soon, for some it comes later. I can say the later the judgement comes the more severe it is.

Luke 1:41 And it came to pass, that, when Elisabeth heard the salutation of Mary, the babe leaped in her womb; and Elisabeth was filled with the Holy Ghost: one more confirmation that there is not just life in the womb, not just the life that God created, there is also a consciousness. A conscience of understanding of the basics of life. A living breathing being inside of an incubator, the mother's womb, to be born once developed. If one has a conscience, he has a soul. You and I have a soul, our soul is who we are. It is what controls our bodies, it is what you are using to read this book and understand what you Are reading. Our souls are our desires, our thoughts. Once you soul leaves your body what happens to your body? It no longer breathes, it no longer moves, it no longer talks, as a matter of fact it immediately begins to decay and rot, what stops a body from rotting, your soul. You souls is your life. Just as we have life so does the baby in the womb.

This chapter has clearly proven that an unborn baby has life, that life begins INSIDE the womb and not outside the womb. If one chooses not to accept what the God of the bible has to say, then they are living in rebellion to him. living in rebellion against the God of the bible, is at the same time to worship the genie god that the world loves so much.

Yes, abortion is one of the most horrible things on the face of this planet, but keep in mind that God loves those that are committing those abortions. God is not willing that ANY should perish. But if they choose not to repent God will have to judge them for their sin. Sin cannot, does not and will not go unpunished, one day we MUST all stand before the God of the bible and answer to him for our choices. Where is your genie god going to be at that time? He will leave you high and dry to suffer all on your own.

BIBLE or TV

2 Timothy 2:15 Study to shew thyself approved unto God, a workman that needeth not to be ashamed, rightly dividing the word of truth.

As we continue on our study of the genie god, the television or TV as it is so commonly called is one of the biggest tools used to not serve the God of the bible. In my opinion the television is a device used by Satan to get people (yes even saved Christians) to fall in love with the genie god of this world. TV is full of sex, lies, violence, adultery, fornication, false religions, false anti-God teachings, and very vulgar language, yet we spend many hours a day watching this junk and filling our hearts with it. My wife and I about 5 years ago left watching cable tv. At that time, it was due to a lack of money, but when we were able to afford it, we chose not to. We found this gave us more time for each other, more time to spend with God, and more time to read the bible. Yes, we do watch some of the streaming channels, but we have learned to be very selective in what we watch, and we do not watch shows with bad content or language in them.

Television has been a tool for many years to influence people. There are a lot of people who have stopped reading their bibles who sooner or later believe in what they see on tv. I was conducting a funeral service the other day for my Aunt who had just passed away. My uncle wanted to say a few words about her (his sister), he said he could imagine her sitting at a table drinking coffee with their mother, he said you know just like you see on tv. We have made our visions of heaven and hell based on tv. I can tell you with truth that if my Aunt was not saved, and I don't believe she was, that she is not sitting in heaven drinking coffee, if she died without Jesus she is tormented, burning in hell where the worm dieth not and the fire is not quenched just as the bible says.(Mark 9:44-48) When we stop believing the bible and stop fearing the God of the bible, we will believe anything that comes along.

About a year ago I read a book by a well know author, this book recorded stories of people who had near death experiences and lived to tell about them. Most of the people in this book claimed to have died and went to another life and then returned. In all of these stories Heaven was described as a beautiful place, with a field of beautiful grass, and children and animals playing, and they saw all their loved ones, and had a great reunion. Then their loved ones told them it was not their time and they had to go back. Toward the end of the book out of about fifty stories there were only a couple of these stories that told of a dark place where it was warm and not comfortable. These accounts of Heaven and Hell can be seen in the TV series called Ghost Whisperer. My wife and I watched that series and all these stories described episodes on that show. Why is this, because the genie god of the world wants people to feel good about themselves, and that it is themselves, not the shed blood of Jesus, that can save them.

I wrote a lot of notes in that book I wrote as the bible says in II Corinthians 5:6-8 that when a saved person leaves their body, they are present with the Lord Jesus Christ. In the book there was always a tunnel that people walked through as well. In Luke 16 the bible tells us that when a lost person dies without Jesus Christ, they lift up their eyes being in torments. This is the story of Lazarus and the rich man. There is no television make nice spin on how comfortable a person will be when they die without Jesus Christ. The genie god makes one believe this garbage and oh what a surprise a person receives when they realize that their genie god told them lies, and that he is now their oppressor.

Do you ever wonder why TV is used so much by the world? It is to get people to believe in man-made ideas of the "after life" and by believing in what a person sees on tv it begins to remove the fear of God from their lives. When a person loses a fear of the God of the bible, they lose a fear of the consequences of their sin, they lose a sense of relationship with the God of the bible, and it makes them want the desire to continue in their sin.

Let's look at a passage in the bible and let's see if TV fits into this passage. If you are one that watches TV that in itself is not a sin, however when a Christian, or any person for that matter, spends more time watching TV than they do on the things of God and the studying the bible, they have opened themselves up to believe this ridiculous non-biblical anti-God stuff you see on TV. I used to say that this would never affect me as I knew what was right and wrong, however I found myself watching only movies that had a high sex content, a high language content, and thought the clean shows if there are truly any left, were boring to watch.

On my road to repentance, I would begin to limit the amount of TV I watched on a daily basis. I used to watch the game show Family Feud with the host Steve Harvey, he was very funny, that show was one I got the concept of and it was a good "family show" to watch. After a while, the Holy Spirit began to convict my heart on this particular show to let me realize that this show was making a mockery of the God of the bible. They were very subtle, and most people would never realize what was going on. Here is what they would do, they would ask questions of families and want them to give the top few answers out of a survey. These questions began more and more to have sexual remarks in them, and then they would have families on there who the dads were Pastors, or deacons in the church, and then when the family, the "Christian" family would answer these questions they would carefully word their answers, and then they would all laugh and have great time rejoicing in the inappropriate content of the question that in no way honored the God of the bible. This is what TV does for the believer who spends more time watching than they do reading or studying their bibles, they become tolerant to sin because it is being fed into their minds ever so subtly. It is time we stop serving our genie god and get back to the bible and the God of the bible. Now to what the bible has to say.

2 Timothy 3:1-17 This know also, that in the last days perilous times shall come. For men shall be lovers of their own selves, covetous, boasters, proud, blasphemers, disobedient to parents, unthankful, unholy, Without natural affection, trucebreakers, false accusers, incontinent, fierce, despisers of those that are good, Traitors, heady, highminded, lovers of pleasures more than lovers of God; Having a form of godliness, but denying the power thereof: from such turn away. For of this sort are they which creep into houses, and lead captive silly women laden with sins, led away with divers lusts, Ever learning, and never able to come to the knowledge of the truth. Now as Jannes and

Jambres withstood Moses, so do these also resist the truth: men of corrupt minds, reprobate concerning the faith. But they shall proceed no further: for their folly shall be manifest unto all men, as theirs also was. But thou hast fully known my doctrine, manner of life, purpose, faith, longsuffering, charity, patience, Persecutions, afflictions, which came unto me at Antioch, at Iconium, at Lystra; what persecutions I endured: but out of them all the Lord delivered me. Yea, and all that will live godly in Christ Jesus shall suffer persecution. But evil men and seducers shall wax worse and worse, deceiving, and being deceived. But continue thou in the things which thou hast learned and hast been assured of, knowing of whom thou hast learned them; And that from a child thou hast known the holy scriptures, which are able to make thee wise unto salvation through faith which is in Christ Jesus. All scripture is given by inspiration of God, and is profitable for doctrine, for reproof, for correction, for instruction in righteousness: That the man of God may be perfect, throughly furnished unto all good works.

2 Timothy 3:1-17 This know also, that in the last days perilous times shall come. Folks, we are living in the last days of this world. Those days may last a few more years, but at some point, the Lord is going to say enough is enough. In this world at the moment, we have a very liberal, democratic government that it is forcing the taxpayer to support the murder of unborn babies in this world. Our tax dollars are going to support the unholy, anti-God agenda of boys and girls changing their gender, they are "allowing" the children to make these decisions for themselves at very young ages. At the end, this is population control, and child genitalia mutilation.

We are being conditioned to accept all this through our televisions. The corrupt news organizations of this nation are feeding daily an onslaught of trash and lies into the minds of the American people and we as Americans are buying this trash. We get our news, our desire to buy products, or longing for travel, and everything from the television. The television is controlled by Satan himself. He uses this to condition people and bible believing Christians, with what he wants them to hear. Satan will NEVER show or tell you the truth at the beginning because no one would go down that road if they knew the destruction that waits for them at the end.

These perilous times are here now, and the genie god is convincing you to accept this stuff and we as Christians are doing just that. When we make the television our primary source of information for our lives, we neglect the bible which should be our only guide to life. If you were to ask the average person walking down the street, and I will say the average Christian who may be saved, and only goes to church some, what Heaven is like, I guarantee you they will describe an idea of heaven based on something they saw on a movie or a television show. There was a book put out a few years ago about near-death experiences, and the stories in this book line up almost word for word with what you see on a television show. Television is what almost all people use to base their religious belief system on. Why is this? Because the genie god of this world wants you feel good and not convicted about your sin. The genie god wants you to serve him while neglecting the God of the bible. The genie god, through television wants you to not read your bibles and rely on the television to provide the word of God through false religions they are promoting.

The genie god uses television to promote the homosexual agenda, we see it in almost every show or movies coming out these days, they make the bible believing Christian soft and a little more tolerant to this kind of an abominable lifestyle according to God. As we have been conditioned to accept sin through our televisions, because we have sacrificed our God time in the bible, we have entered into perilous times. Have you wondered why you never see the bible preaching that is at your church being played on television? It is because the world, through television, controlled by your genie god get offended by the TRUTH of the word of God, the bible.

For men shall be lovers of their own selves, covetous, boasters, proud, blasphemers, disobedient to parents, unthankful, unholy, Without natural affection, trucebreakers, false accusers, incontinent, fierce, despisers of those that are good, Traitors, heady, highminded, lovers of pleasures more than lovers of God; Having a form of godliness, but denying the power thereof: from such turn away. Reading these verses sounds like what happens in almost every movie out there. This kind of sin grabs our attention and gets our interest in the movie or show and we long to see what happens at the end. Watching a movie is not necessarily a bad thing, or watching Television is not a sin as I stated in the beginning of this chapter, however when we neglect our bibles, and our walk with God it will ALWAYS lead to sin.

Here is the thing to watching all these movies and shows, with the selfishness described in the verse above, is that after a while we have no problem watching fornication going on, we become ok with it, it no longer bothers us. We get conditioned to cussing, and vulgar language no longer bothers us, we become tolerant to these little things, and if a person has some kind of an addiction to sex, or drugs, or drinking, they see it on television and have seen it for years and have become very callous to it, it is much easier for them to go down that path. I can speak about that from my own personal experience. There is not one sin described above that is not promoted on the television. The genie god is so happy with people, especially with God's people who have grown tolerant to the promotion of sin right in their very own homes. The genie god loves the fact that parents are training their children to follow after the path of a sinful life that you see on television, and not the Holy life you read in the Word of God. It is truly perilous times, but my friend, it is not too late to make a change back to God. Just unplug your television and open your bible and let the God of the bible convict and restore you back to that Holy life in Christ Jesus.

For of this sort are they which creep into houses, and lead captive silly women laden with sins, led away with divers lusts, I find it interesting that the bible, written many, many years ago, long before the invention of the television, describes how all this sin will "creep" into houses. Almost all bible believing Christians would never allow a prostitute into their home to flaunt her stuff to the men in that household, however they will watch it almost with no second thought on the television. All Christians I know would not allow beer, alcohol, drugs, unmarried sex, or cussing in their homes. But they do allow it to be watched on their televisions, they allow their children to watch it daily, it is promoted, joked about, and becomes a way of life for the television watching person. It is the most hypocritical position for a person to take to say they do not accept this sinful behavior, but then in the very private spot of the homes allow it to be flaunted. If you are against drinking, and do not let people in your home who drink, then unplug your television so it does not CREEP in that way. What we push out the front door we welcome with open arms in the back door. This is what happens when we leave our bibles shut, this is what happens when we worship a Genie god who allows our comfort in sin.

The last part of this verse says that it LED away people in their lusts, the bible uses women, we can also relate that to people. What does it lead them away from? God and the bible. The bible will tell you not to accept any of that at all either in the back door, or in the front door. But we have chosen to worship our genie and reject the almighty. The bible says it is a FEARFUL thing to fall into the hands of the LIVING GOD (Hebrews 10:31)

Ever learning, and never able to come to the knowledge of the truth. Now as Jannes and Jambres withstood Moses, so do these also resist the truth: men of corrupt minds, reprobate concerning the faith. But they shall proceed no further: for their folly shall be manifest unto all men, as theirs also was. Television is a successful key in developing corrupt minds. The bible says here that a corrupt mind will proceed NO further. In other words, your mind will never be able to be focused on the things of God if it is only focused on the things of this world. Television is ONLY focused on the things of this world, and what religious programs there that are on Television are not really bible centered and only preach a watered-down feel-good kind of a God, they preach and teach a genie god, to keep their programs on the air.

The bible says that their FOLLY shall be manifest unto all men, folly simply defined is: lack of good sense. This lack of good sense will become the way of life for the one who makes their life, and knowledge from the worldly television. The poor soul that keeps his bible closed, who only goes to church very little will end up living in his folly that is focused on the Satan serving genie god of this world. The saved Christian who also keeps his bible closed, who spends his free time focused on the worldly television, will also end up living in his folly that is focused on the Satan serving genie god of this world. We MUST get our hearts and minds focused on the things of God. Again, it is NOT a sin to watch Television, however when we put Television before the God of the bible, we then make that television our idol and God says that we are not to have any other Gods before him.

But thou hast fully known my doctrine, manner of life, purpose, faith, longsuffering, charity, patience, Persecutions, afflictions, which came unto me at Antioch, at Iconium, at Lystra; what persecutions I endured: but out of them all the Lord delivered me. Yea, and all that will live godly in Christ Jesus shall suffer persecution. But evil men and seducers shall wax worse and worse, deceiving, and being deceived. Here the Apostle Paul is reminding Timothy about all the suffering that he has endured, he has also reminded Timothy that the Lord has delivered him form that persecution. And that men will wax worse and worse. Wax simply defined is: to increase in size, number, and strength. Evil men will continue to grow, their methods for evil will get stronger and stronger. This is why it is so crucial that we as Christians get into

the Word of God and study it, learn it, and know it, the
Bible says that our faith comes by our hearing, and
learning of the Word of God (Romans 10:17)

The one sure way that is happening today that allows
these people to grow in their promotion of sin is through
the television set. As we said a couple of pages ago,
we would never let the prostitute into our homes to
flaunt their stuff and seduce our spouses, or children,
but we do exactly that by letting it in our homes through
our television sets. It is the exact same thing no matter
how you view it. In an age where evil is increasing by
leaps and bounds, it is crucial for us, for our families,
and especially for our children that we stand on the
things of God. We will all stand before God, the God of
the bible, not the genie god you want to serve, and
have to answer for our own actions, choices, and
thoughts. I will say this, for the saved person that the
bible tells us that the things of God are spiritually
discerned, so therefore we know better, we know what
we are supposed to do, and when we choose not to do
them, we are held doubly accountable (James 4:17)
just remember this, it is a fearful thing to FALL into the
hands of THE living God (Hebrews 10:31)

***But continue thou in the things which thou hast
learned and hast been assured of, knowing of
whom thou hast learned them; And that from a
child thou hast known the holy scriptures, which
are able to make thee wise unto salvation through
faith which is in Christ Jesus.*** Paul says here to

continue in the things which you have learned. He is talking about the things of God. The God of the bible, not this Satan serving, life destroying, sin promoting genie god that hates you and wants you to end up serving in his sin. Get back to the bible. make it a determination to do things in your life the way Gods wants you to do them. Watching television in itself is not bad, and again it is not a sin to watch it, but when it is not controlled the sin of the world will creep in, carry you away from the things of God, and build a tolerance for sin which will be in your thoughts and minds for a while. Again, I am speaking from experience, not just from the bible.

All scripture is given by inspiration of God, and is profitable for doctrine, for reproof, for correction, for instruction in righteousness: That the man of God may be perfect, throughly furnished unto all good works. If you want to grow in your relationship with God than you must get back to the bible. you see here that it is profitable for everything in your life, it will develop a relationship with the Almighty that no man can separate. The bible will make this genie god that you once loved, disappear, and not return again. It will make Satan leave you by resisting him. Satan cannot now, nor has he ever made one single person commit a sin, all he has done is tempted people, he made that temptation look so attractive, so enticing, and the people that fall into these temptations are not seeking the God of the bible with all their hearts, minds, and souls, and that is usually when they get into trouble.

I want to leave you with this challenge, when you are at home, spend one hour a day with the television off, spend that time talking to your family, reading your bible, and praying, do this for two weeks, I guarantee you, you will not miss one single thing in life, but you will gain a little extra peace in your life, a little less stress, and a closer relationship with those you love who live in your home. After the two weeks is up, then increase the time, and after a while the television will no longer be that genie god in your life.

SELECTIVE JUDGEMENTS

This also will be one of those subjects that we truly want to avoid. If you have come this far in this book and have gotten mad, upset, offended, or just plain angry, I can assure you this chapter is not going to help you with correcting that. I cannot and will not apologize for what the bible has to say. If we want to live life God's way, we must make the changes in our lives. If we want to serve the God of the bible, we must first stop serving our genie god, the genie god makes you feel good about your sin, the God of the bible convicts you and makes you feel bad about your sin. It has been said by me many times as a Pastor, the bible will either bring a person closer to God, or it will drive him further away from God, it will bring him closer through repentance, or it will drive him further away through rebellion.

Hypocrisy simply defined is: judging others for what you are doing, and not judging yourself. We often like to have our pet projects that we judge and complain about, but we do the same thing. This is one of those topics that will drive people so far from Christ because we who are the hypocrites are making a mockery of Christ. Do not get me wrong, each person is responsible for their own salvation as you nor I cannot make anyone get saved, but what kind of an example of Jesus have you shown to others, have they seen Jesus in you?

A great example of this was when I was growing up, I went to and grew up in an Independent fundamental King James only Baptist church, and I am pastoring one now. As I was growing up it was back in the era of video tapes also known as VHS tapes. They would have these stores all over where you could go and rent a movie at a cheap rate and bring it home, watch it, then give it back, it was very cheap, and it was the thing that everyone was doing.

We were taught in church that it was a sin to go to the movies. That going to the theater was sinning against

God because you were using the money, he gave you to promote Hollywood and the evil and sin that takes place there. We were in essence promoting a sinful lifestyle that goes against the Word of God. To that point they were correct. It is very sad that we as Christians will promote anti-God stuff in our lives and try to justify it and dig our heels in when people compare our actions to the Word of God. So, at church it was a sin to go to the movies, but it was ok to "rent" that exact same movie and watch it in your own home, in a private setting. The reason the church was against going to the theaters was because going to the theater was promoting Hollywood, so where exactly do you think that VHS tape with that same sinful anti-God movie on it came from, it came from Hollywood. Then it would be said that the money went to the video store and not directly to Hollywood, well, um, where do you think they spend that money at to buy the movies that you are renting? It all goes to the same place. Once again, we were serving our genie god who was making us believe our hypocrisy was honoring the God of the bible.

As we move to today's time we will say "I will never support abortion" I hear people say I will never buy cookies again from a scouting organization because the scouting organization support a national abortion organization which they in themselves are a baby murdering, God hating, Devil serving, people deceiving organization. But these same people will shop at a national retailer who themselves support this exact same organization, so if a person is going to judge, they need to judge correctly. If one refuses to shop at or support one organization for supporting the baby murderers, then they need to refuse to support ALL organizations that do the same thing. The issue is, if we as Christians actually took that stand on all these things we would really need to live like the Amish as almost all organizations especially national organizations support the causes of the baby murders, the gay and lesbian agendas, the organizations that destroy the biblical family, so which is it folks, are we only going to select certain causes to boycott, or are we actually going to boycott all of them? I will shop where I need to get things for my family, I spend the money that God gives me on the groceries, and items we need, once I hand my money to cashier, it is NO LONGER my money. I paid for my groceries. What the organization with their money is none of my business, whether they use their money for payroll, taxes, causes or insurance once I by my groceries or my stuff my money once in their hands is now THEIR money. My point to this is if you don't want to buy your stuff from an organization that supports sinful actions that is fine, but don't buy your stuff from ANY organizations that do the same thing, judge them all the same not just judge some while shopping at others, that my friend is hypocrisy, if going to the movies is sin, then my dear reader so is renting that exact same movie a sin. Also if you choose to not go to one store to shop because of what they support, then to honor the God of the bible you must choose not to support any.

This brings me to one last example before we get to what the bible says. This next example I was told about personally for the husband himself. We were going to our church in Florida. This church had a school, I personally believe that if your church is able to, they should try their best to have one. This man's wife and children were going to the church school, the children were going there as students, and the wife was working there as a teacher, this also provided income for them for their family. There is nothing wrong with working at a Christian school, church, or organization and collecting a paycheck as one has to live their lives as well. This one school year was very difficult for the school itself as there was a lot of worldly influences that penetrated the school and sin was running rampant. The beginning of the following school year this husband decided that his children would be better off in a public school's system because he could not support the sin that was not being dealt with in the school. I cannot say to that point that I disagree with him, I might have done the same thing being in that situation, I can personally say that some of his complaints were justified. So, his position was that his children were not going to attend there, however he was still letting his wife work there because they needed the income. That was a very hypocritical position to take as he could not support the school by sending his children there (which cost him tuition every month) but he had no issues with his wife working in the same school, with the same worldly influence in it, where she was receiving a paycheck. If you can't support one thing due to personal or biblical beliefs, than you must not support it in any manner, even if you gain from that organization.

Churches all across this country will preach out against a church or organization that is not biblically sound, but if that same church or organization made a financial donation to that church, they would accept the money. I know churches that won't associate with other churches because they are not King James bible only, but if the non-King James church made a donation to the KJV only church, they would accept it. One last time, if you are going to be against a cause, an organization, or a person because they do not believe the way you do, or what the bible says, then you need to not support ANY of them in ANY way as that makes you a hypocrite. The genie god of this world loves, absolutely loves, hypocrites, they are his pride and joy, it is because the genie god knows that if he can get Christians to be hypocrites, that it will turn the lost away from the God of the bible, and he will have more people rebelling against God. What this genie, your genie, fails to tell you is the destruction that lies ahead from God's judgement on your life for either a person's rejection of him or their rebellion against him. now onto what Jesus had to say about hypocrites.

Matthew 7:1-6 Judge not, that ye be not judged. For with what judgment ye judge, ye shall be judged: and with what measure ye mete, it shall be measured to you again. And why beholdest thou the mote that is in thy brother's eye, but considerest not the beam that is in thine own eye? Or how wilt thou say to thy brother, Let me pull out the mote out of thine eye; and, behold, a beam is in thine own eye? Thou hypocrite, first cast out the beam out of thine own eye; and then shalt thou see clearly to cast out the mote out of thy brother's eye. Give not that which is holy unto the dogs, neither cast ye your pearls before swine, lest they trample them under their feet, and turn again and rend you.

We will go verse or passage at a time ***Judge not, that ye be not judged.*** This is not saying that we should never judge, a person, this is saying that if you are not willing to be judged by the SAME standard that you judge someone else then it is better that you do not judge. As a bible believing Christian, we must judge sin according to the bible, we must examine a person to see if their actions, thoughts, conversations are in line with the word of God. We are not to condemn them if they are not, we are just to proceed with caution with those folks, remember the saying that if a person is not seeking after God, they will not help you to seek after God. If we do judge a person by the word of God we must FIRST judge ourselves in all aspects to make sure that what we are judging is in line with the bible. if we are not in line with the bible ourselves than we need to get ourselves straightened out first. Jesus will confirm this in the next few verses.

Many people only stop at this verse from the bible, they will say judge not, don't judge me, all the lost of the world know that this is in the bible and will throw it in your face when they are being called out for their sin, they do not want to be judged. When reading and studying the bible you cannot just take one verse and twist it to satisfy that genie god you serve, the verse says Do NOT JUDGE, unless you are willing to JUDGE YOURSELF first.

For with what judgment ye judge, ye shall be judged: and with what measure ye mete, it shall be measured to you again. Jesus says here that we shall be judge by the exact same standard that we judge others by. If you judge someone for cussing and their vulgarity, have you examined your own mouth and your own vulgarity, have you searched your heart to remember how easy it is for you to curse out someone, how about that person that cut you off on the road, did you flip them off or call them a cuss word in your car while you are alone, are you sure you are not just a guilty as the person to who you are rendering judgement to? It is a very tough thing that Jesus is telling us. Are you judging the murdering baby doctor for performing an abortion while you are fornicating with someone, which is the main cause of abortions? Think about this. I am not being mean, nasty, or judgmental, I am just saying, as did Jesus, if you are going to judge a person, make sure you have judged yourself according to the same standard.

Looking at the word "mete" in this verse is simply defined as: giving out by measure. This means the amount of judgement you give to one person or persons the same measure will be given to you. This is where this verse says it shall be measured to you again. That person you are issuing a judgement to will in their heart and mind judge you for the same thing, in the same way, and if the person is not a Christian, your judgements of them can drive them farther away from salvation. We live in a world that is sight based. They see how a person acts and bases that person's beliefs on how they carry out their beliefs. Are people seeing Jesus in you the hope of glory? If we are issuing a judgement against a brother or sister in the Lord, they will be issuing that exact judgement against us, if they find we are not in violation of that same judgement then the Holy Spirit can convict their hearts. Biblical judgement is to judge yourself first, make the necessary changes, then you can help or make judgements against others that are going down a sinful path.

And why beholdest thou the mote that is in thy brother's eye, but considerest not the beam that is in thine own eye? Behold simply defined is: to gaze upon. So, Jesus is asking why do you gaze upon the sin, the mote, that is in thy brethren's eye, but you do not even consider the sin in your own. This is so common in our society today. It is what almost all Christians fight about. I was just taking a break from writing between the last verse and this one for a few minutes and was reading on my social media page of a

KJV pastor who made a comment, and another bible believer did not agree with his comment and instead of them just talking and rightly dividing the Word of Truth, it turned into an argument. I keep my social media page to announce things in the church, to keep up with family, and to promote the things of God. But I do not, I repeat I do not argue with anyone, especially overs social media because if they are dug in and getting angry, they have no desire to listen they just want to be right. In this argument the pastor did what I would have done, he said show me in the bible where my statement is wrong, the other man, a brother in Christ, was calling this pastor names, and making false accusations against him, but this man would not, because he could not, disprove this pastor's statement from the bible. I put this in there as a perfect example of gazing at the sin in someone else, or let's make it simpler, looking at the fault of others while ignoring the faults you have. This is what Jesus is saying here.

Or how wilt thou say to thy brother, Let me pull out the mote out of thine eye; and, behold, a beam is in thine own eye? This is a great question that Jesus asks, how can you help a person to stop sinning if you are sinning yourself, how can you show a person the way to Jesus if you are not seeking Jesus with all your heart, mind, and soul? The last verse was about looking at the sin in another's eye while this one is about trying to tell the person about that sin while having that sin in your own life. This is not necessarily about you and the person you are judging committing the same sin, the brother or sister you are judging for the pride and arrogance that is in their lives, while at the same time you are cheating on your taxes, you are watching that pornography on the internet, yea it is not about committing the same sinful acts, it is about judging sin in another's life, while you are sinning at the same time. Remember the examples we used in the beginning of this chapter, how can you not support one organization which gives their money to baby murderers, while at the same time shopping at another organization that does the exact same thing. Jesus has some very strong words to say in the following verses.

Thou hypocrite, first cast out the beam out of thine own eye; and then shalt thou see clearly to cast out the mote out of thy brother's eye. Jesus calls things just like they are. He calls these types of people, he calls me, he calls you, hypocrites. He makes no mistake in his wording, he holds nothing back, he does not sugar coat his statement, he is honest, and straight to the point, we are all hypocrites when we judge others without first judging ourselves. Jesus goes on to say, get the sin out of your life, focus on yourself first than you can clearly see the path to help others get to God.

Once the sin is out of your life, you have experienced the repentance that is needed, you have understood the forgiveness and the cleansing that I John 1:9 offers the repentant sinner, you understand a deeper form of God's grace, that you can help others find also, through repentance. Why do you suppose that most people will

147

not repent? It is simply because it is difficult to go through, it is a surrendering to God to show you all the horrible, disgusting things you were or are and that surrendering to God will force you to face the consequences of that sin. Most will stay with their pride. Your genie god will do everything in his power to keep you from repenting, he loves it when pride swells up in one of Gods children, he makes you feel so good about your sin, that he loves Pharisees.

Give not that which is holy unto the dogs, neither cast ye your pearls before swine, lest they trample them under their feet, and turn again and rend you. Jesus says this last thing about this, he simply says that when we live in a judgmental state that we are bringing dishonor, disgust, and distrust to the Kingdom of the God of the bible. God absolutely wants nothing to do with our hypocrisy, yet we love it, we live in it, we promote it to others. We are living in a state that God hates. We need to FIRST examine our lives, pray, and seek God like King David did, by saying God please search me, search my heart, and SHOW me the wicked ways that are in me. If you are reading this chapter and getting angry, maybe that is a good place to start, see you are not really mad at me and I am ok with that, you are really mad at the bible, and what it says, you are just mad at the messenger. I know this, I have lived it, I sometimes step back into it, but I am truly seeking God with all my heart and he has to continually show me the sin that is in my life. As I surrender to remove that sin, I get a little closer to him.

This verse simply says by judging others while there is sin in your life you are giving the Holiness of God to the dogs by disgracing his holiness, and furthermore, be careful to whom you give your judgement to, even if it is biblical judgement to because if they are rebelling against God or have a rejection of God, they will try to beat you down, emotionally, spiritually, and sometimes physically. Remember the Lost person will NEVER, EVER understand the things of God until they get saved as the things of God are spiritually discerned. the saved person who is rebelling against the God of the bible will also attack you for telling them the truth about their sin, because they are in that carnal state of mind. You, dear reader, must simply make a choice, to either surrender to the God of the bible and deal with your own sin, or continue to serve your genie god, enjoying the pleasures of your sin but only for a season. Remember these last two thing, number one is we will ALL stand before the God of the bible one day and answer for our actions, and number two the bible tells us it is a fearful thing to fall into the hands of the living God.

FEAR OR FAITH

2 Timothy 1:7 For God hath not given us the spirit of fear; but of power, and of love, and of a sound mind.

In this chapter it is NOT my intent to offend people, but this is likely to happen as we get on this topic. Let me start by saying I am not a medical doctor, nor do I pretend to be one. I am coming from the bible with my comments and opinions. It is my opinion, and only my opinion that most, if not all, diagnosis regarding to any type of mental condition is a result of not seeking God with all your heart, your mind, and your soul. We will discuss in further detail as we get into the verses of the bible.

Take Ritalin for example, Ritalin in my opinion is just an excuse made up for a child's bad behavior. If you take what the bible says, and discipline that child, spank that child when they do wrong, there will be no need for Ritalin. But when a child does not listen, when they choose to rebel against their authority without suffering the consequences, then mom and dad take little johnny to the Dr, the Dr. then decides ok let's medicate Johnny and make him comatose and then he will behave. The Bible says that *Foolishness is BOUND in the heart of a child, but the ROD of correction will DRIVE it FAR from him Proverbs 22:15* did you see what the bible says about little Johnny's actions? It says, if you give Johnny a spanking when he misbehaves, his misbehaving will be driven far from him. This is not something that happens overnight, it may take as in my case, many spankings, but sooner or later the bible will be proven true, and the child does not need medicine, he needs a whooping. Society, through its genie god will tell you that spanking a child is abuse, the bible says it is discipline. Parents you must make your choice, do you follow the bible, or do you follow the world in regard to raising your children, do you spank your child as the bible says, and trust God to fulfill his word, or do you cower in fear of the government and let your child be raised out of the will of God? Just a reminder for you parents out there, it is YOUR responsibility to raise your children, if you turn that responsibility over to the government or medication YOU not them, will have to answer to the God of the bible because he put YOU, not them in charge of raising your children.

I must go on for now and I ask the reader to bear with me as we go through this chapter, I also believe things like anxiety, PTSD, Emotional Support, depression, and all other forms of diagnosis in regard to a person's behavior, are in some ways excuses for these behaviors because of a lack of, or missing faith in the Lord to do what he says he is going to do. Since I have made almost every one of you mad at this point, before you send me the nasty emails, please finish the chapter, but at the end YOU, not me, must make the choice as to whom you put your faith in, it is either the medication of the world, which continues to get your money, or the God of the bible? You not me, will stand before the God of the bible and have to answer for your choices and actions.

Let's now go to the bible and see where I get my absurd statements: ***2 Timothy 1:7-13 For God hath not given us the spirit of fear; but of power, and of love, and of a sound mind. Be not thou therefore ashamed of the testimony of our Lord, nor of me his prisoner: but be thou partaker of the afflictions of the gospel according to the power of God; Who hath saved us, and called us with an holy calling, not according to our works, but according to his own purpose and grace, which was given us in Christ Jesus before the world began, But is now made manifest by the appearing of our Saviour Jesus Christ, who hath abolished death, and hath brought life and immortality to light through the gospel: Whereunto I am appointed a preacher, and an apostle, and a teacher of the Gentiles. For the which cause I also suffer these things: nevertheless I am not ashamed: for I know whom I have believed, and am persuaded that he is able to keep that which I have committed unto him against that day. Hold fast the form of sound words, which thou hast heard of me, in faith and love which is in Christ Jesus.***

For God hath not given us the spirit of fear; but of power, and of love, and of a sound mind. We see the first thing that God, not man, has given us (the saved) is a spirit which is the Holy Spirit. Have you taken a moment and considered what HOLY means? Simply defined is: perfect in goodness, righteous. God, the God of the bible, not this Satan serving genie god, is a perfect God, he is Holy, when we get saved the Holy Spirit comes to dwell inside of us, he leads us to a place of Holiness if we choose to submit to the will of God. So if you ask this question, if the Holy Spirit is leading us to perfection, and we are submitting, then how can there be room for behavioral or mental issues, there can't be. Behavioral, and mental issues are a result of sin, and once the sin is out of a person's life, then holiness can replace that sin and then the results of holiness will be perfection and no more behavioral and mental issues. I do believe that there can be damage to one's mind through the use of drugs or alcohol, and these can affect a person's physical capabilities, I am not talking about this type of a situation, I am talking about that person who uses theses so called medical excuses, while popping themselves full of pills to help control their behavior, because they don't want the consequences of their choices. If you want to try this for yourself, start talking to people who are depressed, or on Ritalin, they will tell you they can't help themselves, they will tell you that is who they are, and some will even say they have a disease and they have to live with it the rest of their lives, to that I say hogwash, as the bible CLEARLY says that God does NOT give us a Spirit of Fear, but of a SOUND MIND.

The next thing in this verse we must see is that through the spirit we have power. This is the power to OVERCOME these issues. It will not be an immediate, or overnight change but a gradual change, as you get more into the Word of God, being around the things of God, hanging out with the people of God, you will find that these excuses the world, your genie god offers you are just that, excuses. When one seeks God and they repent of their sins, and they are intentional to turn back to him, they will, through the Holy Spirit, have the POWER to overcome ANY and ALL of these excuses. If you are reading this and are dealing with some of this at the moment, let me say I am sorry that you are going through this, but have you taken God, completely, one hundred percent at his Word to allow him to make you whole and Holy in your life, or have you just only put in a little effort into seeking him and then gave up because being on that depression medication is much easier and requires much less work? That is what the genie god loves, as he is all about distracting you from serving the God of the bible, the Almighty God.

The next word in this verse is love. Love, true love only comes from having a relationship with the Lord. You learn to love him first, you learn to love him best, and you learn to love him most. He is God, once you surrender to his love and you get his love from him you begin to show that to others. As you begin to show Gods love to others you will see that your problems, issues, and the really bad situations will just somehow seem to be a whole lot lighter. I bet my bottom dollar that any person you talk to that is on medication for some kind of a behavioral or mental condition is NOT reading their bible and seeking God with all their heart. I say it is impossible to have unconditional faith in God if you are surrendering to your pills and relying on your excuses for your bad choices. Again I am truly not trying to make anyone mad, but before you reach out in frustration, try the bible way first. When you learn to love God's way, you will be amazed what is no longer a priority in your life, and you furthermore be amazed by how their worldly diagnosis all of a sudden disappear.

Let's look at the last two words in this verse. Here we go they say of a SOUND MIND. Through the Holy Spirit one has the power of a sound mind. The lost of this world who reject Jesus have no hope at all of ever overcoming these issues, this book is not written to the lost, this book is written o those that are saved, who have accepted the free gift of salvation and are of the carnal mind set, who have a form of Godliness but who are denying the power therof. When one gets saved God gives them the spirit of a sound mind. Sound mind simply defined is: FREE from injury or disease. Uh oh, there it is, it is no longer a disease, it is no longer a medication issue, it is a choice issue, it is a lack of faith in the almighty God. Because he gives you the tools to use to overcome the issues you have. Over recent

155

months I have read and heard stories of prominent pastors who are pastoring big churches who are killing themselves because they were depressed. These are horrible situations, but if a person who is saved is living in a state of depression, they are NOT seeking God as they need to be, they are not taking God at his word. He gives them the Spirit of a SOUND MIND not a fearful mind. Remember at the beginning of this verse he says that he has NOT given a spirit of fear, yet we give into it all the time. We allow the Doctors to medicate us for issues that can be resolved by the power of the Holy Spirit, we allow Doctor to medicate our children for their behavior, when the bible says that we as parents can correct these behaviors if we just do what the bible says to do. The biggest issue is that we have become a lazy set of Christians, who have gotten comfortable in our cozy lifestyles and to maintain that we use any and all excuses to get by. As long as you are willing to use excuses your genie god will continue to provide them for you, and he will make you angry with the God of the bible that tells you differently.

Be not thou therefore ashamed of the testimony of our Lord, nor of me his prisoner: but be thou partaker of the afflictions of the gospel according to the power of God; this address in this passage is from the Apostle Paul to the young Timothy who was left at the city of Ephesus to assist with getting that church there back on track and keeping it focused on the bible and off of what the false teachers are saying. These verses still have the same principles for our topic of discussion. As Paul is telling Timothy not to be ashamed of the testimony of the Lord, nor of Paul and his imprisonment, he is encouraged to be a partaker of the affliction of the Gospel.

I wonder why at times that he was told to be a partaker of the affliction of the gospel. it is because as people hear the truth of the bible most of them will reject it, most of them will hate it, and most of them will persecute the messenger because they hate the message. These are the things that God wants us to have a sound mind for. To get that gospel out into the world which hates it. if one does not have a sound mind then everything else will be a distraction for that person. That bible tells us that a person who is living God's way will suffer persecution. If one is not suffering persecution, it is usually because they are focused on other things. The truth about repentance and service to God is it requires one to be intentional, it requires one to actively seek God. You will NEVER, EVER, have a relationship with God that is prosperous by being lazy, by just sitting around and waiting for something to happen. You must take action to seek God.

Your genie god tells you opposite because he wants you to be lazy, he wants you to depend on others for your support, for your food, for your clothing because all this is in opposition to the Word of God. The affliction we suffer is not to be from an excuse filled Doctor who offers you medication for your laziness and calling you behavior issues a disease, it is NOT a disease, it is simply a choice and which God you want to serve.

Who hath saved us, and called us with an holy calling, not according to our works, but according to his own purpose and grace, which was given us in Christ Jesus before the world began, see that? God, the God of the bible has called us, the saved with a Holy calling, Holy being perfect, without sin. If God has called us to a Holy calling, he will also give us the power to overcome our sin, to overcome our laziness, to overcome our selfishness, we have that power through the Holy Spirit of God to overcome this. As the sin and laziness leaves one's life, it is replaced by faith. As one's fait increases their fear leaves. If you are one to believe everything you hear on TV or the news, I challenge you to turn off that anti-God television and read your bible, study that bible, get out a dictionary and look up the words you don't understand than once you get the meaning go back and read that passage with that meaning in mind and oh what a difference it makes to that study.

But is now made manifest by the appearing of our Saviour Jesus Christ, who hath abolished death, and hath brought life and immortality to light through the gospel: as Jesus brought light and everlasting life to the world, we need to have faith in him to keep us. The bible says that we are to CAST all our care on Him because he cares for us (I Peter 5:7) if we cast our cares on him that would include your anxiety, your depression, your attitude, your victim mentality, it is everything and through the Holy Spirt you have the power to overcome these infirmities. You must make a choice on whom you will serve; continue to serve your feel good, sin loving, God rejecting, genie who will make you feel great for very short time and then leave you high and dry, or serve the God of the bible who will hold you accountable, who will convict you of your sin, but who will also make your life fulfilled, happy, and satisfied while meeting all of your needs here on this earth until we go to Glory.

Whereunto I am appointed a preacher, and an apostle, and a teacher of the Gentiles. For the which cause I also suffer these things: nevertheless I am not ashamed: for I know whom I have believed, and am persuaded that he is able to keep that which I have committed unto him against that day. Paul says he knows whom he has believed in. I will ask you dear reader do you know whom you have believed in. Do you truly trust the God of the bible to not only save you but to keep you, to protect you, to guide you? Do you actually from the depths of your soul believe in that God as much as you should? Once you begin that change in your life, and as long as there is breath in your body, you can choose to go after the God of the bible and forsake your genie god, you will find that your faith will get stronger, and that your fear will depart. These two things, faith and fear are total opposites and cannot exist in the same place at the same time. You will give into one while forsaking the other.

Hold fast the form of sound words, which thou hast heard of me, in faith and love which is in Christ Jesus. As Paul told Timothy to Hold fast, to the sound words, the bible as to which he was taught. Hold fast simply defined is: continue to believe in or cling to. Continue to cling to the bible, continue to believe in the bible and you will find that all your fears, anxieties, depressions, and whatever else excuse with medication that comes down the pipeline will disappear. Because the bible will prove to be true after all. Are you clinging to the words of the bible, are you trusting in the God of the bible, or are you relying on a genie god who has you convinced that this is a lifelong condition and there is no cure? God did not make us to live in fear, a lack of faith creates fear plain and simple.

We will go to one other passage that sums up this chapter. I hope you the reader are still with me in this chapter and have not ripped up the pages, I truly hope that if this has offended you that you seek God first, pray and ask him to show you in the bible where I am wrong before you respond to this. I will leave an email address at the end of the book for comments, but please show me in the bible where God wants people to live in fear?

1 John 4:17-19 Herein is our love made perfect, that we may have boldness in the day of judgment:

because as he is, so are we in this world. There is no fear in love; but perfect love casteth out fear: because fear hath torment. He that feareth is not made perfect in love. We love him, because he first loved us.

Herein is our love made perfect, that we may have boldness in the day of judgment: because as he is, so are we in this world. We see a couple of points to this chapter confirmed in this passage. The first thing is that our love is made PERFECT. When one accepts Christ as their Savior, the Holy Spirit then guides them to a perfect love. How does one get to a perfect love, by removing the sin and weights in their lives that hinder God from doing his very best in your life. Try removing the excuses of these emotional issues and let God replace them with more faith, one receives faith through the bible (Romans 10:17) it will be a struggle, but as you learn to seek God you will find that peace that passeth ALL understanding.

The next thing we see in this verse is "as he IS, so are we IN THIS WORLD" as Jesus is, not was, as he is now, perfect, complete, Holy, the bible says so are we. We are to live our lives in the most Holy way we can, Holiness has no place with sin. Holiness has no place with laziness, or a genie god. Holiness is only associated with the God of the bible. as Jesus is in Heaven so are we, where? In this world. We were never designed to be "disabled" because of depression, or anxiety, or whatever, it is fear and a lack of faith. The best "emotional support" you could receive is from Jesus Christ. He will keep you; he loves you with an unconditional love, he will NEVER leave you nor forsake you, this is his promise, and he is faithful to his promises.

There is no fear in love; but perfect love casteth out fear: because fear hath torment. He that feareth is not made perfect in love. Here is the last nail in the coffin so to speak, Christ loves us, his children, in his love there is no fear, as we love him and learn to make him the most important thing in our lives, our love for him grows, and in the growing love is no place for fear. Where the love of Christ is, there can be no fear. The genie god will never tell you this, he will do his best to hide this from you, the sad part in today's society is that most saved Christians are ok with serving the genie god and living on their medications for their behavioral and emotional issues, because it relieves them from the accountability of their choices. My suggestion is just deal with the accountability, God promised he will walk with you through them, get it over with, get focused on God and you will be surprised how much easier it is to get through. I know you may say that is easier said than done, but this is what the bible says, and yes, it is easier said than done, however if you have the Holy Spirit dwelling in you then you have the power to overcome.

We love him, because he first loved us. How is your love for God, do you love him as much as you love your spouse, do you love him as much as your job? Do you love him as much as your children? To find out how much you love the God of the bible, do this test: write out all the things in your life that you love, including God, then beside each one list an approximate amount of time you spend with each one in a day and see what you love the most. I understand that we have to work, and that requires time, I get that and I am not saying that if one spends forty hours a week at a job that he loves that more, but I am saying that while you are doing your job, and on your breaks, your lunch, what dominates the most of your thought on a daily basis, is it that promotion, that bill that has to be paid? Is it your family, do you spend that time talking to God? If you are focused on God, he will dominate your thoughts most of the day. And as he dominates your thoughts, you will find that things begin to get better as you learn to love him more.

Let me say this again, I am NOT a medical doctor, or a doctor of any kind. I am simply saying what the bible says, and to get you to approach your situation from the Word of God first, before you go to the Doctor. If you are currently on medication for depression, I am not in any way telling you to stop taking that medication, I am simply encouraging you to study the Word of God and see for yourself what the bible says about your condition.

You and only you can make the choices for you. The bible tells us that we will all stand before God one day, we will all give an account of ourselves to him, just remember it is a fearful thing to fall into the hands of the living God. Do you want to stand before God having given your very best to him, I do, for many years in my personal life I rebelled against God and the bible and I praise God daily that he forgave and restored me.

CREDENTIALS and ACCREDITATIONS

All Scripture is given by the inspiration of God...II Timothy 3:16

We live in an age where people have put value in what other people think of them. We value a person based on their education level, we have a tendency to look for letters after one's name and in the ministry world we make one of the biggest mistakes that our generation could ever make is that we require most people who are in ministry to be "qualified" by a man-made accredited college. When you break the whole college thing down to its simplest form all it really is, is an institution that requires you to read books and answer questions on that book for which you pay them thousands of dollars to do so. You could get the books on your own, study them, then be just as qualified to do something as anyone else is. But it requires you to do so. So you pay a college to make you do what you could do on your own if you had the determination to do so.

We have been taught that to be successful we must go to that institution and get a piece of paper with a couple of signatures on it to show that you have higher learning to do a job. In ministry it is sometimes required to have a "Degree" from a college or semitary, sorry I mean seminary before one can preach the gospel or Pastor a church. Nowhere, absolutely nowhere in the bible is it required to go to a college to be "accredited by man" for him to give a God called person permission to Pastor a church. In the Book of Jeremiah God clearly says he will give Pastors after HIS own heart, not asking for man's permission (Jeremiah 3:15) accreditation simply defined is: to give authorization or approval of.

I did my bible college through a correspondence school it was a four-year program; I did receive a bachelor's degree. I am going to be honest, it is nice to have accomplished that goal in my life. Through my correspondence school all my courses were on books of the bible, it required me to read the commentary on that particular book of the bible, then take a test on my understanding of that book. Once the four years were complete it was revealed to me that I could have gotten the exact information from the study of the bible and saved the money invested in it. When a young man surrenders to preach or be a missionary the very first thing that everyone says is ok now you must go to bible college. Please show me a book, chapter, and verse in the bible that confirms that. You will not be able to as it is not in there. To be qualified by the bible to do things for the Lord is to obey. If one obeys then God will lead that person to the resources, they need for the ministry that God has placed them in.

In no way am I saying that going to college or getting an accreditation is sin or against the bible, all I am saying is that the genie god of this world has almost all people convinced that it is required to serve God. There have been many, many churches over the decades that have told people that God has called to preach, or pastor, that the church has said no based on their education, and or other man-made requirements.

When I was seeking God's direction on pastoring a church, I had to fill out many applications for churches and almost all of them required a bachelor's degree or higher, most of them wanted the pastor to have Ph. D to be "Qualified" in that area. We base the calling of God on a person's life by the amount of education they have received. We put people in higher classes of society by their level of education we are very selective. The bible warns us in the book of James about how we classify people and not treat those less fortunate lower than the rich man. If you want to try this for yourself, go talk to your Pastor or any other Christian who has been going to church for a while, and say that you believe you want to preach, almost all of them will say you must go to bible college, they will recommend to you different colleges, but almost all of them will never ask you if God has called you into it. It is all about the level of education. Do you believe that if God calls a person to do something that he is God enough to make sure they receive all the tools necessary to do the job?

How many people in the bible and over the decades has God used to accomplish his will who were unlearned men, who society looked down on? There have been thousands, yet the church today is only focused on education. This genie god as you have seen in the previous chapters of this book is a very smart god as he has gotten God's people to forsake the bible and focus on man-made approval systems for them to share the word of God to others. The great commission does not say go into the world after you receive an education, it says go into the world and preach the gospel. Just study and lean the bible.

We will now shift to what the worldly system of accreditation is basing their authority to overstep God's call, or to give final authority to the call of God on a person. So the first questions are who are the people that have the final say? What makes that signature on that degree valid, what gives them that authority to confirm what you do or don't do? Usually it is a group of people at a college or university that have higher education that will confirm or disaffirm a person's qualification to receive that sacred piece of paper. The best way to describe what I am getting at is to use an illustration. A doctor for example learns the human body as whole, he learns what makes it tick, what is required to heal it, what medication to issue, how to watch for blood pressures and pulses. He learns the human body and makes a living doing that. Then you have the specialist doctor. Who has learned the exact same things to get his basic understanding of the human body but the specialist will go to school longer, he will read more books, and practice and learn that specialty, let's take for example a dentist, he has to learn stitching, blood, mouths, teeth, etc. but as he specializes, he knows more about the teeth and mouth area than a general doctor does because he studies and practices more on that area then the general doctor will. So if one is going to dentist school to become a dentist there will be a board of certified dentist to approve his graduation based on their more intense study than the general doctor had.

This same is true for ministry, if you are called by God to preach, teach, Pastor or whatever, you must go to the bible, it is the foundation of Christianity when a person goes to bible college, they are studying the exact same bible you are they are just studying it more, and putting more time into their learning it. You then have the people who have studied it, may have written books on bible subjects, who "specialize" in certain areas of the bible, because it was of interest to them, they will put even more time into their study and seeking. Just as a doctor will go to college for six years to become a doctor of the human body, so will the surgeon go to school for ten years to learnt he human body but at just at a deeper level. They both started at the same place, but one of them put more time, effort, and focus in than the other one did. We run into trouble when one begins to get letters after his or her name, when we begin to call one pers a doctor and not another. This opens the door for pride to set in. It plows the ground for a haughty spirit. And as a result of the pride and haughtiness it leads man to believe that he can approve or disapprove what God has put into place.

We must remember it is a fearful thing to fall into the hands of the living God. As the doctors in the examples above go to school, they learn from books they read, the same books you can learn from on your own, you can in fact learn more than them, but if you do not have other people who learned the same thing you did, who have a piece of paper that says they know more people will judge you. The bible is clear that we are to judge a person by the fruits they produce in their lives. If a man is preaching and you sense the presence of the Holy Spirit on his preaching than listen to that man, don't focus on his degrees or lack therof, all the degrees say is that he knows what the bible says.

Just another thought as well, a person can go to bible school, get the highest level of education possible, and not have the call of God on his life, if that call is not there than he will not be successful for God as he is doing something that the "church" approves of, but God does not. We must be careful in this area. The genie god loves this when people get to the place in their lives that they know more than what God wants. It is called pride.

Unlike the books we read written by man, including this one that you are reading now, the bible has the authority of God on it. It says it does, it proves it does, so if God calls a person to any sort of a calling that person will find all they need in the bible.

As I write my books, I only use two things on ALL of my books, number one is the King James Bible, and number two is a dictionary to get the meaning of some words. That is it, no other resources are necessary. If we write on subjects on the bible, we are sinful men, and to use another sinful man's work as the basis of a book is heresy in my opinion, we must use the bible. It is good to read other people's books and words, you can learn a lot from them, but don't make their work the basis of your ministry, us the bible and let God get you to where you need to be. To be clear in no way am I saying that other people's books are heresy, I am saying if you base your ministry, or your writings using the resources of other men more than the bible than it is heresy, get your information from the bible, the word of God.

Now to the authority of the bible. *2 Timothy 3:16-17 All scripture is given by inspiration of God, and is profitable for doctrine, for reproof, for correction, for instruction in righteousness: That the man of God may be perfect, throughly furnished unto all good works.*

*All scripture is given by inspiration of God…*this is the most direct statement in the entire Word of God. The bible we have today is inspired by God himself. Inspiration simply defined is: God-Breathed. God spoke every word of this bible. since he spoke it, we can trust it as the final authority. We can make it the basis for judging sin, for seeing the fruits of a person, for hearing if they are sound in doctrine, if they are preaching and teaching the truth. With all the false gospels out there today we must know the bible more to know the truth. ALL, not some but ALL, every word, every story, every punctuation mark, everything in the pages of the bible is God's perfect word, spoken by him. It is final. This does NOT include man made notes in the bible as you have in a lot of study bibles.

and is profitable for doctrine, Doctrine simply defined is: teaching, instructing. The only accreditation a person needs in service for God is the bible. The bible as it tells you here is profitable. Profitable simply defined is: to gain. When a person studies the bible, they begin to gain who God is. Their relationship with God increases. They have that fellowship with him on a deeper level. The Word of God is profitable for doctrine.

As you begin to learn the doctrines you begin to see and hear the false doctrines that are out there. Why is this? Because once you learn the truth of the bible anything that is not truth becomes obvious. Look at it this way, evil would never exist if there were no holiness. How would you compare it to anything? You would never know what is bad unless you compare it too good. The same is true for all the false religions, you must compare them to the doctrines of the bible. This is a personal choice for each person, for me I have made my choice I choose to believe the bible for what it says, I believe every word, every punctuation mark, as the bible says, I believe every jot and tittle. And I compare everything else in life against God's holy word, even the parts I don't like in the bible that tell me I am a wretched miserable no-good sinner who needs to repent. The genie god will only have you to believe and remember the parts of the bible that make you feel good, or the parts that help you to get something from God, like "we know that all things work for good" but the genie god leaves out the rest of the verse. The bible is the only source to gain knowledge through teaching and instruction.

for reproof, reproof simply defined is: Criticism for a fault. The bible will point out sins that are in your life. The bible says that it is profitable in this area. It is a gain in a person's life to have their sin revealed to them so they can repent of their sins and not have anything hinder their walk with God. We live in a day and age that the genie god has gotten people out of the bible, it has detoured people from the word of God that they no longer fear God. People are not ashamed of their sinful choices and in some cases are flaunting in the face of God. This kind of a haughtiness comes from rejecting reproof. It is my belief that there are two kinds of rejection from people toward the bible. there are the unsaved, the bible calls them the Natural Man, because the things of God and the bible are spiritually discerned, they would fall in the first category of jut rejection. Rejection is just a refusal to accept the truth of the bible, and of God. Look at the atheist, he rejects the very idea that God exists. Then there is the saved person, living in a carnal (worldly) state as the bible says, he does not reject God because he has accepted him as his Savior, however he can rebel against God. Rebellion is simply knowing what you are supposed to do and choosing not to do it. this is all part of reproof.

When this verse says that the bible is profitable for reproof it is to make the child of God aware that he has sin in his life. It makes him aware that God is not pleased with the sin in his child's life. So the child of God must remove the sin in his life to get that close fellowship with God. The genie god will convince the child of God that they are ok living in their sin. He tells them that God has not punished them so far so what they are doing is ok. He convinces them that they are free to live life however they want, that they can love whomever they want, that the commandments of the Old Testament were only for them, that when a man laid in a bed with another man that was only a sin back then. The genie god convinces the carnal Christian that they can live however they want because they are still going to Heaven when they die. Why do so many people fall for his lies? Because they have stopped reading, and believing the bible for what it says, they only want to hear the stuff that makes them feel good about themselves, and then blame God for not keeping his promises when their sins catch up with them. This is where reproof is profitable, when the bible points out correction that is needed in a person's life, make that correction, get deeper into the bible, have a stronger relationship with God and you will see the bible to be true after all. The bible simply teaches that our sins block Gods ears when it comes to our prayers. Get the sin out, get God's attention.

for correction, correction has many definitions but for this verse we will use this simply defined is: to bring into conformity with a standard. The bible says that Gods word is profitable for bringing the wandering soul back to God's standard for our lives.

When one is pointed out that they have a fault the bible tells that person that there will be some kind of punishment for their sinful choices, it tells them that repentance is needed, and forgiveness is to be asked for. It is crucial for a person to understand that even though they may have repented and have been forgiven, because the God of the bible is faithful to forgive as he promises to do, that that will not absolve that person for the consequences of that sin. For example, a person kills another person, while in jail they hear the gospel, they accept Christ, they draw closer to God everyday they still have to serve that life sentence, they still have to go to that electric chair, they still have the consequences to pay. For me personally it is relationship with my boys. My sinful choice and pride in my sin, my shaking my sin in Gods face for all those years has caused me a tattered at best relationship with my sons. I have asked their forgiveness but sometimes that does not just wipe the slate clean. That is what correction is about. The genie god will never, ever remind you of the correction that is in the bible, because it does not make you feel good. If you are not in your bible, you will believe this genie god hook, line, and sinker. Blessed is the child of God who repents of their sin, asks forgiveness for their sin, and makes right the best they can the damage caused by their sin, that honors God.

for instruction in righteousness: righteousness simply defined is: acting in accordance with God law. The bible is profitable for the child of God to know how to act. To know what God expects. We often forget that God is Holy. We often forget that part of his love for us is to punish us when we mess up. We often forget that once we became a child of God that we were to live our lives to be holy and acceptable to him. living righteously in this world is not something that just happens, you must be intentional about your walk with God, you must be intentional about seeking God, you must make the choice that you are going to live by the word of God and stay away from that which is against the word of God. When a person believes the bible to be the truth, the whole truth, and nothing but the truth, that is all the accreditation that one needs. You can go to bible college, nothing wrong with that, but all you need to do is get the sin out of your life and get in the word and apply what the Holy Spirit shows you and you will have more knowledge of God than any man-made bible college could ever teach you.

That the man of God may be perfect, throughly furnished unto all good works unlike any and all man-made higher education systems, colleges, universities, community colleges, bible colleges, bible semitaries, etc. only the bible makes a man perfect in the sight of God. The credentials and the accreditations that come from God through his word makes a child of his to be prefect throughly furnished. Throughly simply defined is: complete from front to back. In other word, the bible has all the power and authority from God that if a child of his studies he will be equipped for the business that God puts him in. He will be equipped to live a righteous life, to stand against the false doctrines of this world, to answer questions that the lost or wondering souls will ask, the bible has so much of Gods accreditation in it that it shows only God through the person that lives according to the bible. it is an awesome book. Your genie god can never get you to that point, the genie god will only show you through you, not Jesus through you. The bible teaches that we die to ourselves, and by doing so we become alive unto God.

We will now see the full extent of the authority, the accreditation, of the Word of God. ***Hebrews 4:12 For the word of God is quick, and powerful, and sharper than any twoedged sword, piercing even to the dividing asunder of soul and spirit, and of the joints and marrow, and is a discerner of the thoughts and intents of the heart.***

For the word of God is quick, quick simply defined is: not dead, made alive. The Word of God, the bible is not dead. It is a living book; it is the only book in the entire history of mankind that is alive each and every time one reads it. you can read and study a passage in the bible that you know like the back of your hand, then you can hear that passage preached by someone and get an understanding of that passage that you had not received before, a principle that you had missed. That is what makes the bible alive. The bible says that the things of God, including the bible are SPIRITUALLY DISCERNED. in other words, the Holy Spirit makes them alive. What more authority does one need to believe the bible, certainly not a man-made education system, certainly not a piece of paper with a seal on it to say so, certainly not a group of people to give final authority to what God has put in place. The bible is all that a person needs because it is a living book.

and powerful, Powerful simply defined is: having great power or influence. Since we have determined that the Word of God is alive it also says that it has power. This power comes only from the Holy Spirit working through one's life, because every word is God breathed. When determining the source of one's foundation it is crucial to determine the truth of that particular foundation. As a person goes to a college or University to an "accredited" school it says that that school has the authority behind it to approve or disapprove a person's understanding of that materials they have learned. Unlike all colleges in this world, the bible is designed for the common man to understand. It is designed for the learned man to understand. That is because the things in the bible are Spiritually discerned. when it comes to the Authority of the bible it is from God, made alive by God, and understood by each and every person through the Holy Spirit this is part of the identity of God as God the Holy Spirit. No other book, college, semitary, or whatever could ever possibly have that kind of power backing it.

 and sharper than any twoedged sword, what make the bible sharper than any sword is not that the bible will cut through your flesh, or cut off a limb of a body, unlike the sword the bible, being alive, and God breathed will cut through the soul of the vilest sinner and can turn him to repentance in Jesus Christ. If a sword cuts off a hand that person still has a vile soul inside of a fleshly body that is now missing a hand. Whereas the bible when it cuts to the soul, regenerates the souls which also regenerate how the body performs. I bet your genie god does not care for you enough to show you this. His bible makes you feel all good about you, his bible will never be sharper than any two-edged sword.

piercing even to the dividing asunder of soul and spirit, and of the joints and marrow, asunder simply defined is: into parts. The Word of the living God of the bible will divide the body into parts. Not physically like it separates the soul from the body, that would be death, it will show a person that his flesh is sinful and it has a sin nature, while at the same time his soul has been saved and is now dwelling with the Holy Spirit inside him. this asunder will show a person that through this Holy Spirit, through the Word of God that a person will have the power to control their flesh and be able to resist the devil and his temptations. This also shows that a person can make the choice to serve the God of the bible and to forsake the genie god that has held them in bondage all these years.

and is a discerner of the thoughts and intents of the heart. the bible will guide a person to have thoughts that are Holy and pleasing to God, which will change the intents of his heart to match. There is an old saying out there today, that says before you done it you thought it. before a person commits sin, he has already thought it in his heart. if a person can replace those sinful thoughts in their mind with spiritual thought, their actions will be spiritual.

We will now see that the scriptures that God breathed when the bible was written can still be trusted all these years later, and how it has stood the test of time, stood against all the scrutiny of the lost trying to disprove the bible. I have come across many who question the bible and God's authority over the bible especially the King James bible as to which I am a KJV only person and will not changes on my position. There are many who question the authority of that version, and cling to the "original manuscripts" being the only inspired Words of God, that the versions we have today are manmade and not the perfect Holy bible. I guess you could say they believe in an almost Holy bible, where I believe in a completely Holy bible.

Here is what God says from the bible about his words. **Psalm 12:6-7 The words of the Lord are pure words: as silver tried in a furnace of earth, purified seven times. Thou shalt keep them, O Lord, thou shalt preserve them from this generation for ever.** I hope you have your bibles out while reading this book so you can see for yourself. Never ever just take the Pastors or teachers word for it, make them show you scripture, and you follow along so you can see for yourself.

The words of the Lord are pure words: Pure simply defined is: free from fault. The words of the Lord are pure, perfect, they have no mistakes in them, they have not even a shadow of a doubt in them. Since they are pure, they must be true, since they are true, they can be trusted beyond even the very shadow of a doubt. That's all the accreditation one needs to serve the Lord, you do not need a college education, though you can learn things in college that you can apply to your life in ministry, but it is not necessary. All you need is the bible. The janitor at the local school can have the credentials to tell someone about Jesus because he has a bible that has been accredited by God himself which God has made alive. NO OTHER BOOK could ever do that.

as silver tried in a furnace of earth, purified seven times. Not only are the Words of the Lord pure, but they have also stood the test of time. Many, so very many have tried to prove the bible wrong, and not one of them have succeeded. Many have tried to get rid of the bible, they have tried to stop Christians from talking about God, they have tried with no avail to suppress the spread of the gospel, but Gods Words have been proven over and over again to be true. What makes them so true? They are God breathed; they are inspired by God.

Thou shalt keep them, O Lord, thou shalt preserve them from this generation for ever. As we look at our final section of the verse, we see that not only did God himself give us a bible, he made his words pure, he also keeps his words and PRESERVED them unto ALL generations. God made sure there are bible for his children to live by, he made sure that each and every generation of people have the same bible to read, to study, and to learn so they too can share the light of the gospel to this dark and dying world.

Folks, there is still hope for this world, that hope will still be there until that very moment we meet Jesus in the air in that blessed hope. Until then we are to study, to learn and to tell. Do not get your mind so focused on a college degree, or going to an accredited school, or having a doctorate, these are all man-made status symbols that a person strives for. You have all the accreditation, and credentials you could ever need from the bible. if God has given you a ministry, then get into the word and let him show you what you need. As a reminder, there is nothing wrong with going to a college or bible seminary, or whatever, the issue comes in when we as people begin to "qualify or disqualify" a person based on those credentials or lack therof, base their qualifications on the bible not the man. The genie god focuses on status symbols, the God of the bible does not.

TREASURE

Matthew 6: 21 For where your treasure is, there will your heart be also.

As we get to the last chapter of this book, I actually had about four more chapters but the Lord kind of said no. This one was supposed to be about a social media

Jesus, where we make one post on social media about the Lord, then the very next post has cuss words and vulgarity in it. In regard to social media it is crucial that as a Christian you are very critical of yourself and what you allow on your post because people are watching, they are remembering, and one day they may use it against you. Also you as a Christian are setting a testimony for the Lord Jesus Christ himself. I had an evangelist on my social media page a few month ago, he would post things about Jesus, I also noticed that he would sometimes attack people for their view that was not either in line with the bible, or with what he was saying. It is ok for someone to disagree with you, a person must remember they are not responsible for what another believes or does they are accountable to God for themselves. This Evangelist seemed to me to be more interested in being right, than he was in rightly dividing. I had, over a four-month period, just watched his posts, I had even clicked like on the bible verses he shared. Then this one day he did a post that condemned sin, which he most certainly should have, but the very next post he put on his page in a five-minute period, had the curse words SOB on it. As he called out everyone for their sin, and judging sin according to the bible, it should be called out, I said something along the lines of "one post Jesus, one post SOB?" I ended it with a question mark that was all, he had made a comment on the post to me, before I could see it, he had removed me from his friends list and blocked me so I could not get back to his page. It is stuff like that that I was going to talk about, but the Lord said let's go a different direction.

So we will go on to an issue that covers everyone, rich and poor, small, and great, weak, and strong, male, and female, it is our treasure. In some regards we all have that thing that is our treasure, for some it is a job, for others it is money, for some their families. What we treasure the most in our lives is what we will put our most time, effort, and money into. This is going to be a difficult chapter for me as well because giving is one thing, I thought for a long time I was good at, but I realized over the past few months that I am horrible at giving, especially giving God's way. The genie god will convince you that giving to God's work is ok as long as there is extra money in your budget. That helping a homeless person by giving him cash is a noble thing, the genie god convinces us to tell others that we gave to them. The genie god will also convince us that we can spend three thousand a month on payments for cars, furniture, eating out, movies, etc. but we cannot spend even twenty dollars to put in the offering plate. This is the kind of god I have been serving for a long time now.

It has only been of late that I have dedicated myself to seeking how to be a giver Gods way. I have finally, after forty-six years, started to be faithful to giving to God ten percent of my income. Yes, I am a pastor and I do struggle with complete faith when it comes to my finances. I find it easier to pay the bills with what I can see, then to give some of the money back to God and let him pay them with what I cannot see. My heart has been burdened lately about what we are willing to sacrifice to get what we want. For example, as new to the upstate New York area and moving here to pastor this church I got my job. I work for the same company I have been with for the past four years. I make good money, I have great benefits, I get my bills paid. In Colorado we would use some of our money and get things that were needed for the ministry, as long as we had the money to do so. That if I continue to work this job, I will have to sacrifice some things in the church. I may have to cancel bible study; I may have to post pone things that are part of the ministry to work the job. The bible is clear that I cannot serve two gods. So I have chosen to find a job that only works during the day and to leave the trucking industry as a whole, after twenty-five years working in it. The trucking industry has so many uncertainties. I can be set to get off at four for a church activity and they will come to me at three thirty and say we have to get this last delivery out so now my get off time is after five.

Businesses make their money selling their products. I get it, I understand and the in the delivery business it is how everyone makes their money. After a while I had to ask myself, what is this costing me? It is costing me time for the ministry for what God has called us to, it sometimes costs me time with my wife, as when the time changes and we have daylight longer, it is much easier to work later, for what? money that we are just

going to buy things with that we don't need, to impress
people that we don't like. I have decided I will no longer
serve my genie god of this world and handle my
finances on my own. All that does is get me deeper into
debt. Where the bible clearly says own no man
anything.

I have decided that we will take God at his word in ALL
areas of our lives. That we will do the work he has
called us to do and let him take care of everything else.
We will seek him first and let him make everything else
fall into place. I even went so far as to set up my direct
deposit that ten percent of my paycheck gets deposited
right into the churches bank account. That way it is right
off the top. Since I have shared my sin with you in the
area of complete lack of trust in God with the money,
we will now to go to what the bible says. For me, I could
step out on faith, move across the country twice, as
both times were God led, but I struggle with trusting him
with the little stuff sometimes. This is what my genie
loves about me, I can serve him when I slack on my
trust of the Almighty. Here is what the bible says.
*Matthew 6:19-21 Lay not up for yourselves
treasures upon earth, where moth and rust doth
corrupt, and where thieves break through and steal:
But lay up for yourselves treasures in heaven,
where neither moth nor rust doth corrupt, and
where thieves do not break through nor steal: For
where your treasure is, there will your heart be
also.*

Lay (burden down) ***not up for yourselves treasures upon earth, where moth and rust doth corrupt, and where thieves break through and steal:*** The bible says that we are NOT to lay up treasure for ourselves in this world. When researching some words in the bible it is interesting where the meanings will lead you. I looked up the word "lay", and it has a several different meaning with two different endings. we will examine both of them as it puts this verse into proper context. The first of two definitions is: lay is to set in order, to deposit. The second is to impose a duty, burden, or punishment. The definitions are mainly focused on the burden and punishment part. So let's reconsider this verse for what it says, Jesus says do not burden yourself down with treasures on this earth. Do not set in order or deposit treasures for yourself in this earth. Now this is not saying to not be wise and don't have a savings account but that is between you and God. Remember at the time the bible was written there were no retirement accounts, there were no investments to be made, there was no stock market, there was no need for this because families helped out families. But as the years go on, sin spreads, cultures change, and we have become a society of money seeking people. We have played right into the hands of our genie God. By sin spreading I simply mean, when family no longer supports family, when people have been born with no families to raise them, that soon enough becomes the culture and no longer do we have families raising families.

God tells us not to burden down ourselves with treasures on this earth. We are not to focus on this. Almost all people I know own their homes, I do not. I like renting, I am ok with renting. People in the past have told me that that is stupid to throw away your money on something you don't own. I say but yeah, when the roof leaks, all I do is make a phone call and someone else pays for it, if the a/c unit goes out I just call and someone else pays to fix it. God never called us to own property, he never called us to work our lives to buy houses, cars and whatever to not take a single thing of it with us when we die. The bible does give us liberty to do these things as it is not sin at all to have any of these things. Where it becomes sin is when we have burdened ourselves down with the payments for these and those payments causes us to sacrifice doing or even giving to Gods work here on this earth.

Things will break, rot, or be stolen. Anything man-made has to be repaired, or eventually replaced. That is life, that is because of a sin nature. The bible, with Jesus speaking, tells us not to focus on any of that. This is not an easy task that Jesus asks of us, as husbands and Fathers we have not just us, we have others counting on us to buy food, to buy clothes, to have a good place to sleep. We have responsibilities and we have been conditioned in our childhoods that we must have all this to be good providers. But we have not been taught to rely on God himself as the provider for these things, we have been taught that we must make large salaries, we must have money stored up, we must have this to have that.

All the bible requires us to do is to work to do our part. We are to work, the bible never tells us to sit around and do nothing, we make sure that our jobs do not interfere with our family time, our church time, and especially our God time, you will see that you will have more, you will be happier, and that all the bills will get paid. One thing about chasing treasure on this earth, the genie god will convince you that it is never enough, he will convince you that all you need is a little more, just a little more than you will be set. Have you ever reached that "just a little more" and found that you were not happy, you were not content, because you sacrificed the things of God for the things of this world? When you get a job, ask yourself this, what do I have to sacrifice to work this job? Is Saturdays your time with your family? Then do not work on Saturdays. Are Sundays your days to go to church, then go to church. Are the morning the best time for you to be alone with God then make sure the job does not interfere with that. I truly think those in ministry that have to work, need to find at-home work, or gig work so they can work when they need to, and have the flexibility to accommodate the needs of the family and ministry.

But lay up for yourselves treasures in heaven, where neither moth nor rust doth corrupt, and where thieves do not break through nor steal: For where your treasure is, there will your heart be

also. Heaven is where we are to lay (store up) our treasure. If our focus is on the eternal treasure, we will be blessed beyond imagination. I preached yesterday in church and said that the Apostles in the bible focused on laying up treasure in Heaven because as a result of their work I was able to accept Christ as my Savior many years ago. Just imagine if they had quit telling others about Jesus, imagine if they had served their physical needs and only focused on themselves, imagine if you will for a moment if the Apostles has done evangelism then, like the church does today? The work of the gospel would have failed.

The work for the Lord lasts forever. As long as humans have breath in their bodies, there will always be a need to share the gospel. the gospel brings the most vilest sinner to the cross, it brings the best person on the planet in man's eyes to the foot of the cross. It changes lives. This is what is meant by laying up treasure in Heaven. The spreading of the Gospel, the souls that get saved, the lives that get changes, no one can take that away. Man may try to kill those who are saved, but God always makes a way for some to survive. The ones that do get martyred for the cause of Christ just get to be with Jesus a little earlier than the rest of us. I often tell the folks in the church, the absolute worst that this world can do to a Christian is to send them home to be with Jesus that's it.

Our heart will be where our treasure is. We as God's children get so focused on the things of this world, that we will spend three hundred dollars on season tickets for our sports teams and then rob God of the tithe that he asks us to give as a way of trusting him. we will spend nine hundred dollars on a TV that we will only have for five years or so, but not even give fifty dollars to missions that are seeing souls saved for eternity. These ploys of not giving to God and buying your material possessions that will break, be stolen or have to be fixed, are ploys used by the genie god. Remember the genie god makes you feel good about you. He convinces you that you are to be the greater and the God of the bible is to be the lesser. If you want to prove me right or wrong, look at your finances over the past two months, how much money, have you spent on un-needed temporary material possessions and how much have you given to the work of the Lord which has eternal results? Where your treasure is there will your heart be also.

2 Corinthians 9:6-8 But this I say, He which soweth sparingly shall reap also sparingly; and he which soweth bountifully shall reap also bountifully. There is a direct promise from the Lord himself. He says that if we sow bountifully. Sow simply defined is: to plant seed for growth. If we plant seeds for the Kingdom there will be growth. These seeds are seeds of finances, of time, of spreading the gospel. These are the seeds that God asks us as his children to plant. Nowhere in the bible does God ask us to give of our finances to his work that there is not a promise to follow of him providing more than we plant.

God does not need your money; he wants your heart. if you heart is attached to your money, then God is asking you to give your money to him so he can have your heart. for example, this new church that my wife and I just got called to be the Pastor of, the offerings were low. This church had not been supporting missions for a while. Stepping out in faith I made the decision that as a church we are going to support missions. Since we have done that the offerings have increased a little and are now consistent. We as a church plant seeds, God waters those seeds and makes them grow. I am being honest with you; this is an area of struggle for me. When money seems tight, tithing seems out of the question. All I can say is I have tried for many, many years to pay my bills first which almost always leaves no money for the Lord and I just keep spinning my wheels and getting deeper into debt. I have learned that my way is not working and since I can trust God to be faithful on other things in my life, I am now determined to take God at his word and trust him in my finances. I bet over the next few months I will see a change in our debt load, I will see that there is money for things we need and want, and I will get to experience a deeper intimacy with God. I am putting away my genie god and giving my all to the God of the bible.

As this verse says that if we sow sparingly, we will reap sparingly. This is simply saying that we just give a little to the Lord, he will give a little back, but if we sow bountifully, he will give back to us more than our minds could imagine. Maybe you are faithful in your giving, in you missions giving as well and you have a car payment that is tight on your finances, don't be surprised if one day God send you a check in the mail to pay off that car, or he has someone pay it off for you. Whatever the burden is the Lord knows and if you trust him, you will be amazed as to how he will provide. If you are like me and have been struggling in the area of giving of your finances to the Lord, I do not recommend that you start to give him a lot at the very first as this will only hurt your trust in God, as the testing of your faith in the Lord on the finances you may not be able to bear all at once. I would recommend for a while that you start out with the ten percent and get used to that, then increase it as needed, I also recommend that you give a little above the tithe for missions. Start out trusting small than get bigger as you go. This will build your faith in him stronger. The bible does not teach that we in today times are required to give a tithe. God wants us to be cheerful givers, he wants us to give from our hearts of the increase. But the tithing structure described in Malachi 3 is a great model to follow. It worked for the children of Israel; it will work for us today.

7 Every man according as he purposeth in his heart, so let him give; not grudgingly, or of necessity: for God loveth a cheerful giver. This verse I just referred to. Often, when you tell a person that they need to tithe, or the offering plate is passed they feel like they are required to give. They feel like everyone is watching them to see how much they are putting in that plate. I like the churches that do not pass a plate, ours has a box in the back to put the tithes and offerings in. When a person feels obligated or borderline angry about having to give to the Lord, that is no longer a cheerful giver. You are better off just to hold your money, get your heart right with God and then give. As God loves a cheerful giver. Being a cheerful giver does not mean that you go and tell everyone how much you gave, as you then become a prideful giver. Being cheerful in giving back to God or even to others is a personal cheerfulness, it is a satisfaction in the depths of your soul that you know you are doing what God has asked you to do. It is that peace that passeth all understanding.

8 And God is able to make all grace abound toward you; that ye, always having all sufficiency in all things, may abound to every good as we get to the last verse of this book, we see that God will make all grace abound toward you. It does not say that he might, or that he could, he said he will. He will bless those that give to him from their hearts. He will bless the efforts that one puts into his ministry. If you invest time in your family, you are giving to the work of the ministry as a husband's number one responsibility is to his wife and children. God will bless in all areas that we give for him. jobs come and go, money comes and goes, that's life, so get a job that allows you the time you need to spend with your family, with the service of the lord and let God provide all the material possessions. God is not an unjust God, he is not a mean God, he wants you to be happy and have an abundant life in him. He wants you to have that car you need; he does not really want you to have that payment for that car. Do you believe that God is able to give you a brand-new car for free? I do, if you do than give like getting a new car is no big deal and let God provide one for you. It may not be a brand-new car, but if you wait on him, it will be a paid for car that runs well and that you will have little to no issues with. Because that is how God works. If you go out on your own and get that new car, that is ok also, but then you have a payment that burdens you down. A payment that requires you to sacrifice time with your family, and you're giving to God to make that car payment. Just give to God as he asks and let God be God.

FINAL THOUGHT

The genie god that we have referred to through this book will always lead you to you, and not to the God of the bible. he will make you feel good about your sin, he will convince you that your sin is ok, he will keep tempting you with everything that keeps you away from the God of the bible.

I served this god for many years, I allowed him to be my god, I allowed him to lead my life and all it did was lead me to a place of misery, of distress, anger, bitterness, I could go on and on, but I am not. I am simply saying if you are serving the genie god of this world juts stop. Repent to the God of the bible and start following him in all you do, and you will see how he will change things in your life.

We are in the toughest times that we have seen in while in our lives. Evil is being flaunted in the face of God. It is a very bad day when Gods own children are some of the ones flaunting and accepting sin in their lives. If we as God's children will repent of our sins, he promises that he will heal our land, he will forgive our sins, and he will change the directions that we are heading. It is all about sin. I understand that this book most likely has angered every one of us at some point, I get that, but it is necessary none the less to get the truth out there so we can see for ourselves that we are serving the god of this world and not the God of the bible. Remember we as Christians are held doubly accountable to God for our actions (James 4:17), we will ALL be haled accountable to God for ourselves (Romans 14:12) do you want to stand before the God of the bible and have to answer for serving the God of this world? yea, me neither. So I urge you dear brother or sister in Christ, repent of your sins, turn back to the God of the bible, and let him be the Lord of your life. I will leave you with this last verse. **Hebrews 10:31 It is a fearful thing to fall into the hands of the living God.** For questions or comments please email me at sindestroys@gmail.com   YOU ARE LOVED